Teilhard de Chardin:

PILGRIM
OF THE FUTURE

edited by NEVILLE BRAYBROOKE

 THE SEABURY PRESS · NEW YORK

Preface

Part of this book originally appeared as a section of *The Wind and the Rain,* Easter book for 1962 (London: Secker & Warburg), which is now out of print. Most of the essays have been revised and there are some additions. Grateful acknowledgments must be made to *The Commonweal* in whose pages an earlier version of Madame Dorothy Poulain's piece first appeared (New York: January 30th, 1959), and to the BBC, on whose Home Service "The Vision of Pierre Teilhard de Chardin" was first broadcast in their *Way of Life* series (London: March 22nd, 1964). Other networks interested in relaying this original program must obtain the written permission of the BBC in London. The producer was Fr. Patrick McEnroe and I should like to extend my warmest thanks to him for his encouragement and help in preparing the script.

It is also my pleasure, as in 1962, to extend my warmest thanks first to the contributors for their cooperation, and secondly to many who helped behind the scenes: among them L'Association des Amis de Pierre Teilhard de Chardin, Dr. Lucca Ega, Fr. Robert Francoeur, Dr. David MacManus of the Helicon Press (Baltimore), Mademoiselle Jeanne Mortier, Professor Fooff Ramu, Miss Joan Young, and my wife. I am grateful to Editions du Seuil (Paris) for permission to include work by Pierre Teilhard de Chardin and to the Helicon Press in whose book, *The World of Teilhard de Chardin* edited by Robert Francoeur, the article by Dr. Karl Stern was first published. For permission to reprint the late Fr. C. C.

Martindale's piece, I am grateful to his literary executor, Fr. Philip Caraman, S.J.

Since this book was first set in type, Canon Charles E. Raven has died—a sad loss to Teilhard scholarship.

NEVILLE BRAYBROOKE

London, July, 1964

Contents

The Flare Path of Teilhard de Chardin

An Introduction

Descriptions of Teilhard de Chardin have spread like fire. Some have called him a mystic, a philosopher, a poet, a scientist, a seer, and a seed gatherer. Others have coined longer phrases: a broadcaster of ideas, a naturalist of the open air, and a scholar of bones. He himself referred to his life as that of a wanderer and on many occasions admitted: "I am a pilgrim of the future on the way back from a journey made entirely in the past."

The pioneer must take risks, and Teilhard, whose maxim was "We must dare all," was no exception. Among his coreligionists there were many who eyed his activities with grave mistrust, a mistrust that frequently bordered on fear. "He thinks too much. Such men are dangerous . . ." Before now this has caused others to be regarded with suspicion by Rome—and yet a thinker can never abdicate. "If I didn't write," Teilhard once told a fellow Jesuit, "I should be a traitor."

So, although his religious superiors might prevent his books from being published, they could not prevent them from being written. Nor can a pilgrim of the future grieve unduly if his books appear posthumously, since no matter how much an author may enjoy the praise that his work receives during his lifetime, he knows that what really counts in the long run is the judgment of posterity. In one sense, authors must always remain optimists so continuously must they be sending their words out into the future.*

In Teilhard's case, now that death has freed his books from the ban imposed upon them while he lived, the question to be asked is what has brought them such an immediate and wide response. On publication in Paris *The Phenomenon of Man* sold over seventy thousand copies, and, although its inside story may have attracted some anticlerical buyers, it scarcely explains the enormous sales that have met this and other books of his in France and elsewhere. An author's work that comes out in both French and English may well be accessible to nearly every educated person in nearly every part of the globe, but Teilhard's ideas have quite literally been transmitted even to those countries where the exceptions occur. His soldier's vision of Christ (with which this symposium opens) is a piece of autobiography about the Fourteen-Eighteen War, and has been translated and relayed by radio to eastern Europe and Russia. Moreover its success has led to further broadcasts from his writings on this network.

This success, both far and near, stems from his vision of unity, a vision which has synchronized with a general desire throughout the world for unity. To him, Neanderthal man is no more than a distant cousin just as in his view he accepted "thirty thousand years . . . [as] a mere second for evolution." Pope John the XXIII's short but charged reign introduced a new spirit of good will in a world of differing beliefs where at long last it was recognized that the similarities between most religions are far greater, and much more important, than the differences. In this vision, shared by pontiff and priest alike, charity unites, because charity leads toward understanding and is a foretaste of eternity or what Teilhard calls

* Even this present symposium underwent a certain kind of ban. Originally planned with another publisher in the United States, the American edition was postponed because of the *Monitum* issued on June 30, 1962, by the Holy Office in Rome. In view of subsequent events though, it is worth pointing out that this *Monitum* did not carry Pope John XXIII's signature, and that Pope Paul VI has shown considerable interest in Teilhard's work. It might also be put on the record that, in political circles, the late President John Kennedy was known as "a Teilhard man." "You had better have read *The Phenomenon of Man* before you visit the White House," was a comment often made in these circles.

the Omega point, that final focal point of his where the material and the spiritual will converge.

On May 1st, 1881, Marie-Joseph-Pierre Teilhard de Chardin was born at the Château de Sarcenat in the Puy de Dôme. In this part of France the scenery is dramatic and mountainous, as if the fires of the local volcanoes had burnt themselves into the rock. There is about the landscape a rightness that matches the mood of a child who was later to say: "During every moment that I have lived, the world has gradually been taking on light and fire for me, until it has come to envelop me in one mass of luminosity, glowing from within . . ."

Teilhard saw fire as the symbol of all other forces. It might be the *flashes* of artillery in the trenches; the *sparks* of his own evolutionary quest fanned in his mind by his "dear, sainted maman"; or the *flames* in Hanoi burning a forest to the ground, so that the Chinese might develop it as arable land.

This of course was to see fire in several ways on both a literal and a metaphorical level, or perhaps it would be truer to say on both a literal and mystical level, since for those who can see far enough the first kind of seeing is, if there is sufficient faith, but a preparation for the second. That is why Teilhard has been called a poet and mystic as well as a scientist. He saw as all three.

The whole of life—if not in end, at least in essence—lies in the verb *seeing*, he points out in the foreword to *The Phenomenon of Man,* and it was out of his own particular way of seeing that his vision was born. When a pioneer thinker shares his vision with others, people have a habit of saying afterward: "I can't imagine why I didn't understand that before. But now I see."

Understanding, on all levels, is largely a matter of seeing through things, of penetrating the different layers of existence. When a poet uses words they have layers of meaning, so that sometimes his lines will be saying several different things at one and the same time. Fire may serve him as a symbol of love or destruction, or as a paradox since the same fire that burns can also cleanse. For the mystic, fire may serve as a reflection of divine love, or as a reminder of the burning bush that Moses saw in the desert—although no sharp division can be drawn between the poet's and mystic's calling since the two often overlap.

Likewise, when Teilhard writes that at the antipodes of the fire which unites as love there is the fire that destroys in isolation, and then adds that the whole process out of which the New Earth is gradually born is an *aggregation* underlaid by a *segregation*, he is writing a shorthand that is at once poetic, mystical, and scientific. It is a triple approach which emphasizes the unity of poetic, mystical, and scientific truth, and is a risk in daring that only the pioneer thinker of genius can afford to take. For as the poet and mystic see heaven reflected in the earth—the intensity of their vision being in proportion to the degree that by penetrating the layers of one they can interpret the other, so Teilhard, sharing their vision, sees the whole of creation as a growing state in which a "biosphere" and a "noosphere" are imposed upon the barysphere, lithosphere, hydrosphere, and atmosphere.

"Biosphere" and "noosphere" are words that he coins to convey a layer of living things and a layer of thinking beings—envelopes, as it were, that will gradually enfold the world just as the atmosphere holds the earth in a kind of envelope. In this process he does not see man (who is a thinking being) as a static center of the universe, but as an axis or spearhead of evolution. He is the unfinished product of past evolution and the agent of evolution still to follow, and for this reason, in terms of consciousness and understanding, man has a great deal more to unfold and learn about the universe and himself. That is why Teilhard is so optimistic about the future. The greatest achievements may yet be things to come—in terms of space discovery (a quite realistic project now) and in terms, for example, of the fresh communication that extrasensory perception may make possible between men. (This argument is developed on a later page by another contributor.)

The problem in grasping many of his ideas is their apparent newness. But then new ideas present their own paradox, because since the creation nothing is new, and every seed is begotten by the fruit of another. This may be taken for granted at an agricultural level, but when Teilhard the seed gatherer faces the modern logician in the university there then arises the paradox about the nature of such newness and his vision of God.

For Teilhard, God is the supreme conscious personality in whom all other conscious personalities will achieve union and harmony. He is the God of the future of whom this priest is both a pilgrim and a trail blazer. And yet at the same time he knows that this God of the future has been there from the beginning. To speak of reconciling these two views is to beg the question: only what is separate, or at odds, needs reconciling, whereas for the man whose vision will let him look far enough ahead there is a unity to be found and worked out.

Teilhard's attempts at seeing frequently took him beyond the range of his contemporary scientists and theologians. The originality of his pioneer thinking drew fire on both sides, so that there were times when he was quite isolated and solitary. Lesser men might have given up, or become dispirited. Indeed often he must have had to accept his vision as its own reward—something about which it is so much easier to theorize than practice. For logically, easy enough as it may be for the believer to accept the truth that the more a man extends his awareness of his place in the universe, the more his adoration of God will grow in depth, so running parallel with this acceptance will be the knowledge of those spiritual troughs of despair in which any man of prayer may be caught. Nobody can come away from reading either Teilhard's letters or journals without realizing the tremendous inner struggles that must have taken place. Some writers create a spiritual hush in the mind —and there are many passages in Teilhard's books that do this. After reading them, there comes a feeling that life can never be interpreted in quite the same terms again.

This experience is the mark of a classic in any sphere, and the diversity of commentary that follows such work is often a tribute to the diversity of its nature. It is worth remarking on the enormous number of different types of books in which T. S. Eliot's name is listed in their indexes; it is a sign of his range of influence —and something similar now seems to be happening with Teilhard. Neither italics nor inverted commas are necessary for the term the wasteland, so much a part of accepted speech has it become. Maybe the same acceptance awaits the term the "noosphere."

The contributors to this volume about Teilhard's life and work have by no means covered all the aspects of his thought. Their contributions are better regarded as points of departure, like this introduction. . . . There are however one or two matters which can be cleared up on the reappearance of this symposium in a revised, separate, and extended form.

Some reviewers of the first edition called Teilhard "a Catholic deviationist." The late Father C. C. Martindale, S.J. (who is represented here) rebutted this charge once and for all in a letter he wrote about his friend to *The Times Literary Supplement.* Here is the relevant extract from it:

From my many talks with him, I am entitled to say that he never meant to assert, or even think, that there was any "break" with, or even "discrepancy from," Catholic orthodoxy, in his view of human existence, though he knew that what he said (including his annoying neologisms) would be surely misunderstood. I often said to him: *"Please* don't be so exasperating!" He'd say: "Mais, mon petit, il faut parler comme on peut!" He was quite sure (as I am) that he never meant to deviate from any of the great Catholic dogmas in which he wholeheartedly believed . . .

This needs stressing because Teilhard was no Tyrrell.

Another matter that should be mentioned concerns the piece included on "Teilhard in Fiction." Some have seen in Romain Gary's picture of Père Tassin in *The Roots of Heaven* (1956) a portrait of Teilhard; others, a pale shadow. The French editor of Teilhard's *Letters from a Traveller* says in a footnote that the portrait is "so distant . . . as to be unrecognizable." But the fact that the editor felt compelled to add this footnote is perhaps not without significance. In my discussions with the contributors, I have found that they take a divided line on this issue.

In assembling the symposium, two letters have lain at the top of my file. One comes from Mrs. Renée Haynes (a pioneer herself in the field of extrasensory perception) and adds its own footnote, as it were, to comments made by other of his friends:

I met him briefly with Sir Julian Huxley in the 1950's. . . . The thing that struck me most about him was not his brilliant intelligence, which I took for granted, but the sense of goodness, almost of holiness, which seemed to go with him. He was quiet, but seemed to have a strong sense of humor: I remember gray eyes and a thin figure. I do not mean that I perceived any physical fragrance about him; if I had I should probably have attributed it to hair oil or something. No, it was an "atmosphere" (what Hindus call the *durshan*) which came with him. My own conclusion would be that he was very much a man of prayer.

The other letter comes from the late Miss Augusta Mullikin of Texas, and refers to the 1930's in Peking:

I was a fellow guest with Père Teilhard at a small dinner party. . . . When a large roast goose was carried in, he said in a teasing way: "Is this perhaps the great American eagle?" Our hostess was an American. His manner and expression was gracious and playful.

These two aspects—the playful guest and the man of prayer—have been sadly lacking in some portraits that have been painted. But all those who knew him testify to them. He no more wanted to force his life into a series of separate compartments than he wanted to force all men into one mold, or to regard science and religion as unrelated facts of experience. Nor did he accept the conventional dichotomy between mind and matter.

In his view, matter and consciousness were the outward-facing and inward-facing facets of the same reality. Further, he believed that the inwardness of reality had been asserting its independence of the outwardness, and that the world was slowly groping its way, as promised, toward the communion of saints. But the promise he accepted not merely as scriptural, since he also saw it as the logical outcome of his own scientific research. No wonder then that he thought of all research as adoration, thus bringing out, incidentally, a fresh meaning from the old Latin tag, *Laborare est Orare*.

To others pursuing the path that he blazed it would be foolish to maintain that he succeeded in uniting all the facts of evolution with the supernatural elements in Christianity, since a great deal more remains to be done. But a gallant clearing has been made, and Teilhard, like a true pioneer, would have resisted exaggerated claims for his achievement. He himself always had the modesty to allude to much of his writing as "essays." *Le Milieu Divin* he describes as "an essay on the interior life," and on four occasions in *The Phenomenon of Man* he refers to it as "an essay." This is its own lesson, and it is in this spirit that the sketches and essays presented here have been written.

Part I

Teilhard de Chardin Speaks

1

Christ in Matter

By Pierre Teilhard de Chardin
Translated by Noël Lindsay

My friend is dead. He was one who drank deep from life, as from a holy well. His heart burned within him like a flame and his body has been swallowed up in the earth outside Verdun. Now I can hand on some of the sayings by which he initiated me into the intense vision which illuminated his life and brought him peace.

"You ask," he said, "how it happened to me that the whole mighty and manifold universe took on the likeness of Christ. It came about gradually. It is hard to find words to analyze intuitions of that kind, which make all things new. But I can tell you some of the experiences which let the light in upon my soul, as though a curtain were lifting by fits and starts."

THE PAINTING

". . . At that time," he began, "my mind was full of a question, half philosophic, half aesthetic. Imagine, I thought, that Christ vouchsafed to manifest himself before me here, in the body, what would he look like? How would he appear? What would be his way of enfolding himself perceptibly in matter? What would be his impact on the things around him? . . . There was something disturbing, something shocking, in a confused way, in the idea that the body of our Lord could mingle in a mundane setting with the throng of meaner bodies around him, without their experiencing and recognizing by some perceptible change, the intensity at their side.

"It happened that my eyes fell mechanically on a painting of Christ offering his heart to mankind, a painting that was hanging before me on the walls of the church where I had gone to pray. And, following my line of thought, I found it hard to understand how a painter could depict the sacred humanity of Jesus without making his body seem too specific, too absolute and thus seeming to isolate him from all other men, without making his countenance too individual, and, even if he gave it beauty, giving it some particular beauty which excluded all other forms of beauty.

"Thus, I was pondering deeply on these questions and contemplating the painting, when the vision began.

" (Although, in truth, I can hardly tell the exact moment when it did begin, for it was already quite intense before I became aware of it.)

"What is certain is that, as my eyes wandered over the outlines of the image, I suddenly observed that they were *melting*. They were melting, but in a manner very special and difficult to describe. When I sought to discern the lines of the person of Christ, they seemed to me to be sharply drawn. And then if I relaxed my attempts at vision, the whole outline of Christ, the folds of his robe, the radiance of his hair, the bloom of his flesh, merged, as it were, but without vanishing, into all the rest. . . .

"It seemed as though the surface that separated Christ from the world about him was changing into a film of vibration in which all limits were confounded.

"I think the transformation must have started somewhere near the borders of the portrait and spread from there until it embraced the whole contour. At any rate, that was the sequence in which I became conscious of it. From that moment, in any event, the metamorphosis spread fast and overtook all things.

"The first thing I noticed was that the vibrant atmosphere which surrounded Christ with a halo was not confined to the small space immediately about him, but that it radiated to infinity. It was shot through from time to time by what appeared to be phosphorescent trails, tracing a continuous path of light as far as the outermost spheres of matter—making a sort of plexus of blood vessels or network of nerves throughout all substance.

"The whole universe vibrated. And yet when I tried to look at things one by one, I found them still as clearly defined, their individuality still preserved.

"All this movement seemed to emanate from Christ, from his heart above all. But it was while I was seeking to descry the source of the emanation and to capture its rhythm, that my attention came back to the picture itself and I saw the vision mount rapidly to its climax. . . .

"I forgot to tell you about the garments of Christ. They were luminous, as we read in the account of the Transfiguration. But what struck me most was the realization that they were not woven by art—unless the hand of the angels is the hand of matter. . . . Those were no coarse spun fibers which made up the weft. But matter, the very flower of matter, had woven itself of its own accord in the inmost of its substance, like some miraculous tissue. And it seemed to me that the stitches flowed indefinitely, harmoniously combined in a natural design, destined for them from their first beginning.

"But you will understand that I had only a casual eye for this garment miraculously woven by the continuous cooperation of all the energies and all the order of matter. It was the transfigured countenance of the Master which attracted and captivated all my attention.

"You have often seen, by night, how some stars change their color, from pearls of blood, to violets of gleaming velvet. And you have seen the shifting iris on a transparent bubble.

"Thus, in an inexpressible iridescence there shone on the changeless countenance of Jesus the lights and tints of all our beauties. I cannot tell whether it was at the behest of my own desires or at the will of him who ruled and knew my tastes. What is certain is that these innumerable shades of majesty, of gentleness, of irresistible attraction, succeeded each other, were transformed and merged into each other with a harmony which appeased me to the full.

"And always behind this shifting surface, supporting it, concentrating it in a higher unity, there floated the incommunicable beauty of Christ. . . . That beauty, too, I divined rather than perceived.

For whenever I tried to pierce the layers of inferior beauty which
concealed it from me, other particular and fragmentary beauties rose
up which veiled from me *the True Beauty,* while making me foresee
and desire it.

"The whole countenance was radiant in this way. But the source
of the radiance and the iridescence was hidden in the eyes of the
transfigured portrait.

"Over the profound splendor of those eyes there passed, like a
rainbow, the reflection (or it may have been the creative form, the
idea) of everything that charms, everything that lives. . . . And the
luminous simplicity of their fire resolved itself, as I endeavored to
master it, into an inexhaustible complexity, in which were united
all the looks in which a human heart was ever warmed and mirrored.
Those eyes, for example, at first so gentle and tender that it might
have been my mother before me, became an instant afterwards as
passionate and subjugating as those of a woman—and yet so im-
periously pure that under their dominance no false feeling was
physically possible. And then they were filled in turn with a great
and manly majesty, like the look you can read in the eyes of a very
brave or a very strong man, but incomparably more lofty and more
delightful to undergo.

"But while I was ardently gazing deep into the eyes of Christ, and
saw them become a bottomless well of fascinating and blazing life,
lo, from the depths of those same eyes, I saw, as it were, a cloud
mounting, which overcast and engulfed all that I have just described.
An extraordinary and intense expression spread gradually over the
changing shades of the divine countenance, first impregnating them
and then absorbing them.

"And I stood dumbfounded.

"For this ultimate expression, which dominated and summed up
all the rest, *I could not decipher.* I could not say whether it betrayed
unspeakable agony or an excess of triumphant joy. I only know that
since then I seem to have discerned it once again in the eyes of a
dying soldier.

"At once my eyes were veiled with tears. And when I could see
again, the painting of Christ in the church had resumed its too sharp
lines and its motionless features."

*   *   *

"My spirit had always been naturally pantheistic," [1] continued my friend. "I felt its inborn and unconquerable aspirations, but I did not dare to give them free rein because I could not reconcile them with my faith. After these experiences and others like them, I can safely say that I have found a life-long unexhausted interest and an unalterable peace.

"I live in the heart of a single element, the center and the detail of All—personal love and cosmic power.

"In attaining it and merging myself with it, I have the whole universe in front of me, with its noble endeavors, its entrancing search for knowledge, with its myriads of souls to be perfected and healed. I can and must plunge breathlessly into the midst of human labor. The greater share I take, the more weight I will bring to bear on the whole surface of the real, the nearer I will attain to Christ and the faster I shall grapple myself to him.

"We could say that God, eternal being in himself, *for us* is in the process of formation everywhere around us.

"And God, too, is *the Heart of Everything.* This is so true that the vast setting of the universe might founder or perish or be snatched away from me by death without diminishing my fundamental joy. When that dust is scattered that was made animate by a halo of power and glory, there still remains untouched the reality of substance in which all perfection is subsumed and incorruptible. The rays are refracted in their source, and there, all converged, I would still hold them.

"That is why I am not disconcerted, even by war itself. In a few days we shall be hurled into an offensive to recover Douaumont— a magnificent feat, which I see as the symbol of a positive advance of the world in the liberation of souls. I tell you this. I shall go into it religiously, with all my soul, borne by an impetus in which I cannot tell where human passion ends and adoration begins.

"And if it should be my lot not to come back from those heights, I would like my body to rest embedded in the clay of the forts like

[1] A very real pantheism (in the etymological sense of the word: *En pâsi panta Theos,* that is, in Saint Paul's words, *God all in all*), but an absolutely legitimate pantheism; for if, in the last analysis, Christians are in effect no more than "one with God" this state is reached not by identification (God becoming all) but by the differentiating and communicating action of love (God all *in all*)— which is essentially orthodox.—*Footnote added by the Author.*

a living cement which God has cast between the stones of the New City."

These were the words which my dear friend spoke to me one October evening, the man whose soul was instinctively in communion with the unique life of all things and whose body now reposes, as he wished, somewhere in a wild land.

1916

2

The Meaning and
Constructive Value of Suffering

By Pierre Teilhard de Chardin
Translated by Noël Lindsay

Illness, by its very nature, tends to give those who suffer from it the impression that they are no use, or even that they are a burden on the face of the earth. A sick man is almost inevitably bound to feel that, in the main stream of life, he is, by sheer misfortune, set apart from all the endeavor and all the stir; his condition seems to have no sense; in the midst of universal action it seems to doom him to inaction.

The object of the following reflections is to try to dispel these saddening thoughts by showing, from a tenable point of view, the place and efficacy of suffering in building the world, even the visible world itself.

BUILDING THE WORLD

First and foremost, the world is still building.

That is the basic truth which must be grasped at the outset and assimilated so thoroughly that it becomes part of the very habit and nature of our thought. At first sight we might be tempted to think that created beings and their destinies are dispersed at random, or at any rate arbitrarily, over the face of the earth. We could almost believe that each one of us might equally well have been born earlier or later, here or there, richer or poorer, as though the universe from start to finish of its history were some vast pleasure garden in time and space, in which the gardener could change the flowers about at his own sweet will. But ideas of this kind will not hold water. The more we reflect, in the light of the lessons to be learned from science, philosophy, and religion, each in its own sphere, the more we realize that the world is to be likened, not to a gathering of individual elements, assembled with art, but rather to some organic system, animated by a broad movement of growth, special to itself. Over the centuries an all-embracing plan seems in truth to be unfolding around us. Something is afoot in the universe, some issue is at stake, which cannot be better described than as a process of gestation and birth: the birth of the spiritual reality formed by the souls of men and by the matter which they bear along with them. Laboriously, through the medium and by virtue of human activity, the new earth is gathering its forces, emerging and purifying itself. No, we are not like the blooms in a bunch of flowers, but rather the leaves and blossoms of some great tree on which all things appear in due season and due place, in time with and at the behest of the All.

THE MEANING OF SUFFERING

It may be thought that this conception of the world in a state of growth is ingenious but abstract. In fact it has immediate practical consequences, since its whole tendency is to give new strength to our mental concept, either of the value of individual human effort (enhanced by all the universal labor with which it is united) or (and this is all that concerns us here) of the price of individual human suffering. Let us expand this point a little, bearing in mind the comparison between the tree and the bunch of flowers.

In a bunch of flowers it would be surprising to find imperfect or sickly blooms, because they have been picked one by one and assembled with art. On a tree, by contrast, which has had to fight the internal hazards of its own growth, and the external hazards of rough weather, the broken branches, the bruised blossoms and the shriveled, sickly, or faded flowers are in their rightful place; they reflect the amount of difficulty which the trunk which bears them has undergone before attaining its growth.

Similarly, in a universe where every created being formed a small self-contained whole, willed for its own sake, and theoretically transposable at will, we should find some difficulty in justifying in our own minds the presence of individuals painfully cut short in their possibilities and their upward flight. Why this pointless inequality, these meaningless restrictions? . . . In contrast, if the world really represents a conquest still under way, if at our birth we are really thrown into the thick of the battle, then we can well understand that, for the success of the universal effort, in which we are at the same time the partners and the stake, pain is inevitable. The world, looked at empirically on our scale, is an immense groping, an immense search, an immense attack; it can only progress at the cost of many failures and many casualties. The sufferers, whatever the nature of their suffering, are the reflection of this austere but noble condition. They are not useless and diminished elements. They are merely those who pay the price of universal progress and triumph. They are the ones who have fallen on the field of honor.

THE CONSTRUCTIVE VALUE OF SUFFERING

Let us go a little deeper. In the entity formed by mankind as a whole, and subordinate to Christ in the "mystical body," there are, as Saint Paul tells us, different functions, different members. What member can we conceive to be more specially charged with sublimating and spiritualizing the labor of progress and conquest? The contemplatives and those who pray, no doubt. But also, very certainly, the sick and the suffering. By their nature, by their complexion, the sufferers find themselves as it were driven out of themselves, forced to emigrate into the present forms of life. Are they not therefore, by that very fact, predestined and elected for the task of elevating the world above and beyond immediate enjoyment toward an ever more lofty light? It is their part to tend toward the divine more explicitly and with greater purity than the rest. It is their part to give breath to their brothers who labor like miners in the depths of matter. Thus it is exactly those who bear in their enfeebled bodies the weight of the moving world, who find themselves, by the just dispensation of providence, the most active factors in that very progress which seems to sacrifice and shatter them.

THE CONSEQUENCE: THE CONVERSION OF THE WORLD'S SUFFERING

If this assessment is right, the sick man, in his apparent inaction, is faced with a most noble human task. No doubt he must never cease seeking betterment or cure with all his might. No doubt he must employ his remaining strength in the various forms of work which are still open to him, sometimes very fruitful. It goes without saying that Christian resignation is the very converse of capitulation. But once this amount of resistance to evil is secured, the sick man should understand that, to the very extent of his sickness, he has a special task to fulfill, in which no one else can take his place—namely, to cooperate in the transformation (it might be called the conversion) of human suffering.

What a vast ocean of human suffering is represented by the whole of the suffering on earth at any moment! But what makes up that mass? Blackness, deficiency, waste? No, we repeat, but rather potential energy. In suffering is concealed, with extreme intensity, the world's power of ascension. The whole problem is to liberate it by making it conscious of what it means and what it can achieve. What a leap forward the world would make toward God if all sick people at the same time converted their pain into a common desire that the reign of God should rapidly mature through the conquest and organization of the earth. All the sufferers on earth uniting their suffering so that the world's pain became a great and unique act of conscience—would that not be one of the highest forms which the mysterious work of creation could take in our eyes?

And is it not exactly for that reason that creation, in the eyes of the Christian, is consummated in the Passion of Jesus? We are perhaps apt to see nothing more on the Cross than individual suffering and expiation. The creative force of that death eludes us. If we looked with a larger view we should see that the Cross is the symbol and the focus of an action whose intensity is inexpressible. Even from an earthly point of view, fully understood, Jesus crucified is not outcast or defeated. He is, on the contrary, the one who bears the weight and bears always higher toward God the progress of the universal advance. Let us do likewise, that we may be united with him all the days of our life.

1933

Part II

Comment on Teilhard's Life and Achievement

3

Enfance Prédestinée

By Claude Cuénot

Une immense fleur de feu. Sur la blancheur du crépi, c'est un éclaboussis de rayons. Les yeux graves et doux de la mère se penchent sur l'enfant, si bien que l'aurore, le regard de la mère et l'âme du petit garçon échangent leur lumière. L'enfant joint les mains pour prier l'Enfant-Dieu: Déjà tout, dans sa vie, devient plus embaumé, plus coloré, plus pathétique. Déjà, il devient sensible à l'éternel sourire de l'univers.

Un paysage calme et pensif où des Puys géométriques: demi-sphères, parallélipipèdes, cônes et troncs de cônes, découpent l'horizon avec des nettetés, la saveur d'absolu d'une épure. Leurs opalescences émergent de la plaine sur quoi flotte une brume sans limites, tandis que jaillissant du décor vert jade des pins et des acacias les hirondelles ricochent sur la tour à poivrière.

Une enfance heureuse, telle est la force de l'homme. Pour ceux qui furent des enfants comblés, le refuge restera toujours de remonter dans la mémoire: A Sarcenat, le matin, que l'air est doux! Mais la fin du jour est plus tendre encore lorsque les arbres s'effrangent sur un ciel bleu perle frappé de nuages gris. Charme vaporeux des après-midi sur la plaine, et des roses brouillards de l'automne.

Une enfance heureuse, qu'anime entière le besoin de posséder, en tout, quelque absolu, mais parfois traversée, dans son unique pas-

sion, de gros chagrins comme les ombres légères des nuages sur la
terre chaleureuse: une boucle de cheveux que happe une flamme
tapie dans les bûches du foyer, le Dieu-Métal, cette clef de charrue
soigneusement dissimulée dans un coin de la cour, et qui rouille
et se raie . . .

Une enfance déjà dévorée par la passion de l'inconnu et du
nouveau—qui, sous un ciel d'encre et de cuivre, poussera le petit
Pierre à s'échapper à l'aventure au long des pentes foisonnant de
tritomas, parmi les constellations de lis jaunes et rouges, de prime-
vères écarlates et d'iris—qui induit son âme, à l'heure où s'allume
la multicolore féerie des signaux, à suivre l'élan des grands trains
vers un matin prestigieux et enchanté.

Child of Destiny

Translated by Isobel English

An immense burgeoning. On the whiteness of the rough-
cast walls, it is like a splashing of rays. The serious and gentle eyes
of the mother are focused on the child, so that the break of day,
the mother's look, and the little boy's soul merge their light. The
child joins his hands to pray to the Son of God: already everything
in his life has become more sweetly scented, more heightened in
color, more poignant. Already he has become aware of an eternal
smile in the universe.

The Puy countryside, out of which geometric shapes emerge,
seems calm and reflective: half-spheres, parallelepipeds, triangles,
and truncated cones cut the horizon with mathematical precision
—a taste of the absolute given by a diagram. Their opalescence
emerges out of the plain's endless mists, whilst swallows rising out
of the jade-green backdrop of pines and acacias ricochet over the
pepper-pot tower.

An untroubled childhood is the life-giving force of man. For those with a childhood crowned with happiness, there will always be a shelter to return to in memory: at Sarcenat, how mild the air is in the morning! But the evening is even sweeter when the trees are fringed by a pearly blue sky stamped with scattered gray clouds. O vaporous charm of the afternoons on the plain, of the pinkish mists of autumn!

An untroubled childhood which is quickened in its depths by the desire to possess, in everything, something absolute, but which sometimes, in its unique passion, encounters great setbacks like the dappled shadows of passing clouds on a summer landscape: a lock of bright hair snapped up by a tongue of flame circling round the logs in the open hearth—the God of Iron, that key of a dismantled plow carefully hidden in the corner of the courtyard, getting rusty and cut to the bone.

A childhood, early devoured by a passion for the unknown and new, which once, when the sky was inky black and copper-colored, drove little Pierre to venture out of the house on his own along the slopes stocked with a mass of tritomas, among yellow and pink lilies, dark red primulas and irises, like constellations of stars. A childhood which, when the multicolored enchantment of the railway signals is being lit, inspired in him the desire to follow the departures of the heavily-laden trains toward an elusive and magical morning.

4

A Geologist in the Field

By George B. Barbour

It was my privilege to be in the field with Père Teilhard de Chardin on four continents—in eastern Asia, where for a decade we explored in a dozen of the provinces of China, often with no other white companion—in California, in the company of other geologists—in France, in districts more familiar to him than to me —and in the Transvaal, whither we went at the request of the Wenner-Gren Foundation on the invitation of the men who had come upon the fossil remains of the Australopithecine man-apes, buried in the breccias of refilled fissures in limestone. It had been planned for us to join the University of California Expedition to South Africa in 1947, when a heart attack prevented his going and I had to go alone. But four years later he had recovered sufficiently for us to be able to visit the most critical localities together.

Teilhard had reached China and started on his work with Père Emil Licent at the Musée des hautes Etudes when I first met him in 1923. Father Licent liked to make expeditions into the "back lots" of the northern provinces along unfrequented routes, to add to the natural history exhibits in his museum in Tientsin. Licent's record of his journeyings was compiled from field journal entries, dealing mainly with day-to-day occurrences on the road, with little or no attempt to interpret, or to find underlying unifying principles in the observed geological facts. Accounts of his journeys were published accompanied by large sketch maps, based on compass readings taken at each bend of the road, with distances measured or estimated between villages or road junctions. The scientists traveled with a Chinese cart, a driver and a cook-boy. As anyone who has used that agonizing means of transport knows, the wise voyager can easily keep up with a Peking cart on foot, with much greater physical comfort. Père Licent knew the radius of the wheels, painted a mark on one of the spokes, and measured the distance traveled by counting the innumerable turns made by the wheel beside which he was walking. At intervals the cook's slumbers were interrupted, he was evicted, and the scientists took his place. From that point on, distance was judged by time elapsed, as the beast seldom exceeded ten Chinese li per hour on the level. In China, distances are apt to lack the rigid precision of our western units. The li has a pleasing elasticity. It measures about one-third of a mile on the level, but places seem farther apart when you are walking uphill than when the gradient is with you. As a unit of effort therefore it may be farther from X to Y than it is returning downhill from Y to X. And on an uphill grade the speed of the cart fell below eight li per hour. When a village ahead looked like promising a respite, with a chance for a drink of well-water or tea, the mule and the driver exerted themselves to a spurt of twelve li.

When Teilhard shifted his base to Peking and became attached to the Cenozoic Laboratory, we made our reconnaissances in the same way, though whenever possible we took also two Mongolian ponies and a second muleteer. We were also sometimes fortunate in having with us one of the young Chinese geologists. At times it was C. C. Young, a vertebrate paleontologist, trained by Schlosser in Germany, who worked with Teilhard in the Cenozoic Laboratory and who was with us on the expedition up the Yangtze. Once or twice it was Edward Mei-nien Pien, the geomorphologist from Yenching University, who joined us on the Honan trip across the Tsinling range. On at least one occasion it was L. C. Li who had worked with me in the Kalgan and Nihowan districts.

Teilhard used a minimum of equipment and carried only a small black notebook with *quadrillé* pages. I used colored pencils to distinguish formations, but he insisted that a pencil or stylo was enough. The rest was stored in his head. The pencil was usually blunt and was often licked. In the field he wore a khaki drill suit of military cut with four pockets—the upper ones for pencil, pen, cigarettes, and matches, and the lower pair for the little black notebook and for his breviary. I think his pocketknife, hand lens, and military compass went in a hip pocket.

His tall spare figure covered the ground with a steady, alert step, faintly uneven because the right foot was turned out a little more than the left. Nothing of geological importance missed his eye. Riding a Mongolian pony across gravel-strewn terrain in Jehol, he could spy a reworked stone implement fifteen feet away, where others saw nothing but a spread of pebbles. Along the bank of the Vaal River in Orange Free State he spotted two waterworn paleolithic hand axes in a layer that was supposed by the local archaeologists to have been picked dry. At the infamous Piltdown gravel pit he found a single tooth after many others had searched the spot.

For some unexplained reason, Pierre never made any attempt to learn the vernacular and knew only half a dozen words of Chinese. In consequence he was at the mercy of whoever was his interpreter at the moment. My own grasp of the language was definitely colloquial but sufficed to make purchases, buy railway tickets, bargain for help at fords, find quarters in an inn, arrange with military or police officers from whom we had to secure permission to pass through their areas, or even to gain entry to a walled town after dark.

He was an ideal field companion on the 1,700-mile expedition we made from Shanghai up through the Yangtze gorges to western Szechwan. Little work had been done on the Pleistocene history of the Red Basin and it fell to us to carry through a project planned by the late Dr. Davidson Black, whose tragic death on the eve of our departure deprived us of the inspiration of his enthusiasm. I had already reached Hawaii on the way to join them in Shanghai when the sad word came. Teilhard suddenly found himself called on to assume under peculiarly difficult circumstances the interim directorship of the Cenozoic Laboratory, established with Rockefeller assistance by the Geological Survey of China following the discovery of *Sinanthropus* (Peking man). A better understanding of the Pleistocene history of China called for more data bearing on the evolution of the land surface in the peripheral zone of the region which had Peking at its center. We had already done work in Manchuria, Jehol, Outer Mongolia, the Ordos and across northern China to west of Lanchow. The second main drainage artery from the west, that of the Yangtze Kiang, had to come next. On those trips we used virtually every mode of travel—rail, river steamer, sampan, airplane, horse- and donkey-back, ricksha, sedan chair, truck, bus, model-T Ford, Peking cart, even coolie-back across the Wen Ho, and of course hundreds of li on shank's mare—everything, in fact, except camel and water buffalo, because to broaden our experience we even once went half a mile in wheelbarrows equipped with sails in the Honanese manner. We decided that progress on foot was less hazardous!

Except when planning to stay overnight at a mission station or rest house where our arrival was anticipated, we tried to reach a village before dusk and find quarters either in the court of an inn or on the k'ang, or mud platform, on which all guests of the local caravanseries slept in rows, or on the stage of an open-air village-theater, or in a temple building. While we set up our canvas camp cots and washed, the cook lit a fire, boiled water, and bought eggs and noodles in preparation for the evening meal. Our supply box added tea, sugar, condensed milk, chocolate, confiture of some kind, or a small tin of fruit. For emergencies it also had bully beef. When darkness fell we had only the feeble light of a candle. After writing up our field notes for the day, we would discuss the day's results and the problems that lay ahead before crawling into our sleeping bags and extinguishing the light to avoid attracting mosquitoes. Pierre would feel in a breast pocket for his packet of Job or Caporal cigarettes, and I would pull out my pipe. During the daylight hours in the field, his mind and talk had concentrated strictly on the business in hand. But when night fell, he would talk freely, relaxed and content, about the ideas close to his heart, and his mind would reach out into the future. What is the solution for the increased overcrowding of the world? How should men deal with the inter-group tensions that prevent them from living peaceably together? If material progress carries men forward and religion leads them upward, should we not somehow combine these in a resultant? Does the noosphere hold part of the answer? . . . until one or other said, "Bon nuit! Dorme bien!" and we fell asleep. At the time, much of what he said was beyond my grasp. I have often wished since that I had recorded some of the conversations of those nights under the stars, since in them lay the germ of many ideas which were later fully developed in *Comment Je Crois, Reconstruire la Terre* and *Le Phénomène Humain.*

Mankind falls into two groups—the vast bulk, which thinks with the times, if not behind them, and the small group with the vision and power to think ahead of the rest. The influence of the inspired thinkers in the latter company depends in part on the extent to which they are in advance of their time, and in part on how far their contribution can build on the thought of others among their contemporaries. In rare instances the individual is a catalyst of ideas that are breaking to the surface in many places around the world. Darwin's insight was of this type—an instance of the right man being in the right place at the right time. History provides other examples of such prophetic leadership. Père Teilhard's contribution is comparable. It will be some years before the full impact upon human thought of the ideas of this modern scientific mystic is truly appreciated. Like other great spirits he was very human and approachable.

Such a seer with a gifted pen faces the risk that his disciples read into what he has written interpretations based on their own particular experiences. Teilhard himself was disturbed by the way this had been so in his own case. He felt, for instance, that extensions of ideas to which he could not subscribe were being attributed to him to a degree that distressed him. Later, he welcomed the months in his study up under the roof of the Wenner-Gren Foundation in New York City as a chance to revise and rework his earlier essays, so as to minimize the misinterpretations that had been rife after some of his writings had been copied and broadcast in France without his sanction in the years immediately following the war. For his ideas had come at a time when disillusionment was widespread and they offered a new hope to thinking men and women in a generation whose faith had been undermined by prevailing materialism.

Teilhard was always generous in giving full credit to others whose ideas he adopted. He was troubled at being credited mistakenly with the discovery of the *Sinanthropus* skull which was actually found by W. C. Pei. His own very significant contribution lay in the determination of the mammalian fossils unearthed from the same layers as Peking man, which were important in trying to date the deposit and reconstruct the environment.

While strict with himself, Teilhard was always amazingly tolerant of human failings in others. He always had a kindly interpretation of any weak brother's actions. When the mule, carrying his baggage was fording a tributary of the Han, suddenly decided to sit down and try to roll in two feet of water, drowning all his possessions, Teilhard turned distress into comedy. We spread our garments on bushes along the river bank to dry for two hours in the hot sun of a baking July day. "Le pauvre bête must have welcomed that refreshing bath."

According to my dilapidated field notebook, it was on Tuesday, July 24, 1934, that we pulled into the courtyard of the *yamen*, or magistrate's palace, at Lu-shih on the Lo-ho River in western Honan. We had left the railway at Lo-yang two days before. From the excitement and curiosity that greeted us in the villages along the way, we were evidently the first *yang-kwei-tze*—"foreign devils"—to enter a region which for several years had been bandit-infested and was regarded as a hornet's nest. The Nanking government under Chiang Kai-shek had just cleared the area, and appointed keen young military officers to restore order and these had not yet fully taken over their new duties. The pass across the Tsinling range was still not considered safe for travelers and we had been directed to the military headquarters to present our credentials, and be granted access and safe conduct. The new command had arrived so recently that we were their first official guests and had arrived even before the buildings had been swept out. The new district commander felt obliged by the laws of courtesy to offer us hospitality and kept us in the outer court while he made the place presentable and prepared a meal to welcome us. We had been on the move since leaving Ku-hsien at 8 A.M., and had wasted at least an hour getting the cart and ponies across a ferry. It had rained and we had only covered some fifteen miles of thoroughly bad going. Pierre sat down on the stone steps of the *yamen* to rest and await developments, and watched the efforts of some soldiers to unload their gear from the back of a balky mule. One of the men shouted in Chinese that the beast had a nasty temper, but the remark was lost on Pierre. He was still commenting on the applicability of an inscription by Li Po which Young had translated from a stone tablet in the Red Basin earlier in the summer. "It is as hard to travel in Szechwan as to go to heaven." Just at that moment the men dropped their load and the mule struck out with a hind leg hitting Pierre on the temple. The blow broke a blood vessel and within a few minutes he had a dark blister the size of an egg right over the temporal artery. Within five minutes we had commandeered the nearest room in the outer court of the *yamen* and his camp cot was set up. Ice does not exist in a Chinese village in July, and the medical orderly of the post had no supplies of any kind except a little ether. Through the night I kept Pierre's temple cool with constantly changed compresses. I read to him from the little breviary he had been using in the cart earlier in the afternoon, and waited in fear for the dawn. But his one concern was for "ces pauvres gens" who had prepared the meal with such care, with no guest to partake of it. By morning the swelling was distinctly reduced and he tried to insist on going ahead. But I pointed out that the mule had prevented my writing up the conclusions on the previous day's traverse, and that the chief of police said we must not proceed until a messenger had gone ahead to warn the outposts of our coming.

Two days later he was in fit condition to travel. The path had become so narrow that the cart was paid off and dismissed, and we put our baggage on mules, the muleteer in Chinese fashion counterpoising the weight of the baggage by three heavy stones, to keep the load in balance. Pierre always preferred to travel with a long metal military kit-box for his maps and most of his kit, beneath which he hid the tin tubes in which were stowed some two hundred Chinese silver-dollar pieces—the only currency that was always good in face of the devaluated vagaries of unlimited paper money. Two days later we threaded the pass over the summit of the Tsinling range.

On the southern face of the range the descent was down a winding gorge so narrow that the footpath had to cross and recross the river at every bend. The fourth day started with a four-kilometer stretch during which we had forded the current, waist high, thirteen times. The number must have struck the baggage mule as unlucky, the ill-balanced load having begun to slip, and as it neared the bank the beast tried to lie down and roll, but managed first to drop the kit-box and bedroll in two feet of water. We bathed. For the next hour we sat on the bank with clothing spread on the bushes until the sun dried out the other soaking contents from which Pierre had surreptitiously removed the hoard of dollars. I have preserved a memento of the occasion. The river was so deep that we had had to cross half-naked with our clothes and shoes in a bundle over our shoulders. I had a rucksack which made for easier crossing and had reached the bank ahead of Pierre in time to catch him, on my last twenty feet of ciné film, stripped and washing off the mud. I left China before it could be developed, and it lay for two years unseen in the Cenozoic Laboratory in Peking before reaching me in New York. When I showed it to Pierre fifteen years later he remarked: "Do you think le chef de mon ordre, if he saw this, might not consider me to have been unfrocked prematurely? Tell me, George, did you ever anywhere find colder water than in that miserable river?"

5

Memories and Letters

By Lucile Swan

My first meeting with Père Teilhard de Chardin quite changed my life. Shortly after I arrived in Peking in the autumn of 1929, I was invited to a dinner of scientists at the home of Dr. Amadeus Grabau, the geologist. The whole "gang" (as Teilhard used to call them) were there—V. K. Ting, Wong Wen Hau, Davidson Black and, of course, Père Teilhard and Grabau. I was immediately impressed by this tall ascetic priest who was so alive and so gay; there also radiated from him a spiritual quality that everyone sensed immediately. I was delighted to be placed next to him at table, and almost at once we were engaged in serious conversation. Speaking as a scientist, he said that the deeper he went in science the more sure he was that there was a God. This seemingly self-evident statement was like a light to me. I had been an ardent Episcopalian when young. I had married an artist, and I belonged to a world of artists in which no one believed in anything beyond his own work and efforts. I had drifted away from all formal religion. Yet those simple words of Père Teilhard's made a tremendous impression, and roused a great hope in me. It was the first of our many talks, and the beginning of a long correspondence about philosophy and belief.

We were a strange and motley group of people in Peking of

many nationalities, professions, and interests. Among the important diplomats, scientists, writers, and artists, always Père Teilhard stood out in any group. One felt his radiant and loving presence. Even the most hardened felt his spiritual quality and wanted to be near him. How many who would not have approached an ordinary man of the Church, went to him for help, and always found it, for he talked to them in language that they understood and could act upon. I remember so well a Jewish friend whose life was quite broken by family difficulties, and who had also drifted away from her early training. "But you have a beautiful and rich heritage," he said to her. "Why don't you study your own religion and you will see how much help there is in it for you." Not long ago I found her reading a 'Life of the Early Prophets' with great enjoyment. "You have no idea," she said, "what a beautiful and helpful tree has sprung from the seeds Père Teilhard planted so long ago in Peking." Her experience could be multiplied dozens of times.

I shall quote from letters over many years which may give at least a fragmentary expression of the development of his beliefs.[1]

In July, 1933, he wrote from the steamer on his way to the United States: "I have the obscure feeling that something is moving and growing in me: as if in the course of this new period of complete freedom the true 'myself' was escaping still from the world of conventions. This new and direct contact with the unbelief of the world makes me more sharply conscious of what I believe (strongly) and what I do no more believe (equally strongly). . . . But what to make of that? . . . My dearest faith is that something loving is the deepest essence of the growing universe." And then he enclosed what he called his creed.

I showed it to him not long before his death and he said it quite adequately expressed what he still believed. I give it here:

> We cannot be fundamentally happy but in a personal unification with something Personal (with the Personality of the Whole) in the Whole. This is the ultimate call of what is termed "love."
> Hence the substantial joy of life is found in the consciousness

---

[1] I should add that Père Teilhard usually wrote in English—though if the subject was very abstruse he would go into French. [There are some curious idioms used in these letters—but they have been let stand. Editor.]

or feeling, that by *everything* we enjoy, create, overcome, discover, or suffer in ourselves or in others in every possible line of life or death (organic, social, artistic, scientific, etc.) we are gradually increasing (and we are gradually incorporated into) the growing Soul or Spirit of the World.

This feeling supposes only that we have a passionate human heart, and that we admit in addition the three following points, namely:

1. The Evolution or the Birth of the Universe is of a *convergent* (not of a divergent) nature: toward a final Unity;

2. This Unity (gradually built by the work of the World) is of a *spiritual* nature (the spirit being understood *not* as an exclusion, but as a transformation, or sublimation, or a climax of Matter);

3. The Center of this $\frac{\text{spiritualized Matter}}{\text{spiritual Whole}}$ therefore has to be supremely *conscious and personal*. The Ocean collecting all the spiritual streams of the Universe is, not only something, but *somebody*. He has, Itself, a face and a heart.

If one admits those three points, the entire life (including death) becomes for each of us a continuous discovery and conquest of a divine and overwhelming Presence.

This Presence enlightens the deepest secret Zones of everything and everybody around us. We can reach it *in the achievement* (not in the mere enjoyment) of everything and everybody. And we cannot be deprived of it by anything or by anybody.

Later that same year from Paris he wrote: "The fundamental bearing of my life is to prove to the others and firstly to myself, that the love of God does not destroy, but exalt and purify, any earthly power of understanding and loving. I dream of going to God under the pressure of the strongest and wildest spirits of the world."

Early in January, 1935, on his way to southern China, he wrote from the ship: "My dream is that we could be a little like a star each for the other, by the presence as much as by the absence. A star, leading to the best of the Unknown, in front of us. You know how much I feel that the only important work in the world is the discovery (or rather the creation) of the future. Now, can it be a more vital line in such a progress than to discover a new path and a new ground for the power of love?" Also from that same trip, dated January 28, at Kweilin, Kwangsi, he describes the countryside in another letter: "From a picturesque point of view we are in one of the most famous and strange places of China. All around Kweilin, and far south, the country is a forest of high pillars or needles of limestone (about 80 or 90 meters high) forming a most extraordinary landscape. These are the remains of a highly dissected limestone plateau. Amongst the maze of fantastic rocks emerging from a brick-red soil, the river runs, a transparent jade-green water. The pity is only that the country is so much deforested. Here the vegetation is not so tropical as in Nanning—no more palms nor cycas in the rocks. But still we are in a country of oranges, mandarins, and pomelos. The weather is cloudy and almost cold. The houses are mostly open and there is no fire except for fire-bowls." He had written earlier from Nanning: "People look frozen and go along the roads under blankets or with small baskets with burning charcoal on the belly. It is a pity to see the country without sun, everything is so tropical; the huge green trees, the fruits, the red soil, the ferns, and the bright birds."

Some months later, back in Paris again, he wrote: "I have but little doubt that I am going to reach a new level of 'passion for the world,' and a fighting optimism. But the 'assimilation' of new elements has first to be achieved, before I can clearly see in the spiritual world, in front of me. I need a renewed expression of myself. I will get it from a renewed faith in life." And a few days later: "Everything seems to be an impossible mix-up, at present, in the world. Yet, every day brings me a new evidence that we are playing our part in the birth of something great. I think that, at no other time, has tension for life been so strong."

That autumn he left France for India, where he joined Dr. Helmut de Terra in a scientific expedition. From the steamer, he wrote: "My present topic is more and more *L'union différencie*. There is a full metaphysics, ethic, and mystic, contained in those three words." Later in November, in Rawalpindi, he writes: "Here the conditions are simply exquisite. Two days ago in the bad lands, I had the most beautiful evenings of my time in India. The sun was gold over the yellow and pink clays of the desiccated desert—over the dry grass and the thorny trees of the bush; just like firm white clouds in the blue sky of the East, the snowy lofty Pu Panjal (the last born Himalayan range) were floating above the landscape. And troops of green parrots were passing too."

Further south in India, he again writes: "A golden light was spread over a lovely country, thickly spotted with huge evergreen trees, mangoes, banyans, etc. On both sides of the valley the tabular masses of peninsular India's ranges covered with dense jungle, a tiger jungle! You could see peacocks flying in the woods, a few crocodiles in the river, and lots of dark-faced white-bearded monkeys everywhere in the bush and along the roads. Native people exceedingly clean and amiable, the men with white cloths and turbans, the women all in pink or scarlet veils, much better looking than in the Punjab. Geologically we had a grand time."

In 1936, as I was making a trip up the Yangtze, he wrote from Peking where he had been visiting Monsignor Commisso, who had asked him to write a confidential report which could be sent privately to some high officials "at the heart of Rome." He comments: "I was startled by the idea, and I think I will write the thing, very shortly, and with the appropriate tune, but very frankly. My idea," he continues, "is to choose as a title *Réflexions sur le Conversion du Monde* (because the pages would be sent first to the Commission de la Propagande), and then to expose why (and how) we need to propose a new side of the 'old' God, and a new type of worship (based on adventure and discovery).[2] The substance would be the same as in 'Christ and Evolution' but with slightly subdued expression (and yet perhaps a clearer and more direct focusing on the question)."

In looking over these old letters, I realize what a busy life he led. In the summer of 1936, he made a trip along the coast of Shantung, and in 1937 he was back once more in Paris.[3] Always he was hard

[2] I often heard him repeat that the time would come when the important divisions between men would not be into nations, but into those who believed and those who did not believe.

[3] During his trips to France he had long talks with his superiors in his Order, who feared his ideas were too new and dangerous in their innovations. "I try to bring the attention of the authorities to what I think is happening in the world at this moment," he wrote to me on one occasion. "The appearance of

at his scientific work, but would say: "The real interest of my life is no longer in past rocks, but in the modern world." A letter written in June, 1937, states: "Crowning my growing convictions and 'admiration' for Human Energy, I discover more clearly, just now, the tremendous value and 'function' of the 'Love of God' (well, understood, of course) for building the human world; 'Love of God,' which has been chiefly studied, so far, as an individual relation between man and the summit of the world—but which has now to be understood as the highest and most universal form of spiritual activity. By this wonderful type of psychical energy, every single other form of activity is increased and overanimated; a natural agreement becomes possible between totalitarian tendencies of human society and the achievement of personality (love is the *only* strength which makes things one, without destroying them); and finally, a possibility is open for controlling (without diminishing) the fundamental power of human love. A chapter on these considerations will surely be the end of my next essay on Human Energy. . . . Everybody is thinking of Totalitarianism and Personality just now. Politically Europe (even France) is just a volcano. Everybody is now awake to the urgency and *to the size* of the human problems; and the necessity of finding a practical solution to difficulties *obliges* the most conservative people to face a thorough recasting of the ancient conceptions of the world. Something is obviously coming to birth. On the other hand, 'impersonal' totalitarianisms (Communism, Fascism . . .) prove failures. Positively, I do not see any natural escape but in the direction of a Personalistic Universe. My faith in a neo-Christianity is growing stronger every day. So, you see, I am not losing my time. A degree more of contact with the Center is more important than any progress in the knowledge of past geology." A little later that same month from Puy de Dôme, he adds: "In this restful environment I have the impression [sic] to 'expand' internally, and I become conscious of a kind of new light which

---

a new faith in man, without which the Christian faith loses its power of contagion, of consolation, and of defense against the new humanisms (Marxism, to start with). All I want to say can be summed up in three phrases. 'Some—the old-fashioned Christians say: Await the return of Christ. Others (the Marxists) reply: Achieve the world. And the third (the neo-Catholics) think: In order that Christ *can* return, we must *achieve* the world.' "

has been burning in me in the course of apparently somewhat dis-
appointing weeks in France. Never before perhaps did I perceive
so clearly the possible meaning of the evolution of my internal life:
the dark purple of universal matter, first passing for me into the
gold of spirit, then into the white incandescence of personality, then
finally (and this is the present stage) into the immaterial (or rather
supermaterial) ardor of love. And never before, too, did I realize
in such a tangible way how much people around me are starving
for the same light, which perhaps I can transmit to them. For several reasons (including the fact that younger generations are gradually emerging over the older ones, and also the marvelous and critical conditions of a world which is facing for the first time the real
dimensions and risks of its destiny) I was never received before by
my friends with such frank sympathy, and almost 'expectancy'!
Maybe something will come out of the seeds which you help me to
spread, some day not too far ahead. I had to miss a lot of opportunities these past weeks; and yet as a final result, I feel *myself* more
than ever. Is it that I needed to be somewhat cut from science and
the past in order to perceive more distinctly the higher precincts of
the coming universe?"

After some months he was back in Peking,[4] and in January,
1937, he was off on a scientific expedition to Burma. From the
steamer, he wrote: "I have decided to use the first part of the journey for making my 'retrait' . . . I somewhat miss my notes and
familiar surroundings . . . And yet to be practically alone on the
sea, and bound for action, is a favorable atmosphere for perceiving
the best of God. Many points seem to appear more simply and more
distinctly in my mind."

And then from Burma came this beautiful description of the

---

[4] In Peking, I remember, we often took walks in the parks of the Temple
of Heaven or by one of the lakes of the Forbidden City, which, since the
Republic, were open to the public. In "Central Park" were enormous pottery
bowls containing unique goldfish, such fish as only the Chinese could have bred.
They were beautiful and terrible, gold, gold-brown, and blue-silver, with great
pompons over their bulgy eyes, and with tails and fins nearly a foot long which
looked like the finest chiffon. Père Teilhard would explain how these mutations
had been brought about and what they would lead to. Or, on another occasion,
he would scratch a bit of bark on an old tree to expose a tiny insect, and would
then proceed to tell of its life and habits, especially of its seventeen-year hiber-
nation period.

country: "After a few days spent near a very majestic volcano in the plain (Mount Popa) we have migrated to the Shan Plateau. Very cool weather, and such magnificent scenery; huge green forests, on which spring spreads creamy and pink touches, and eventually flame-colored patches. Two days ago we motored on a precipitous road, to the deep valley where the Salween River runs parallel with the Mekong. A few miles further were the first slopes of Yunnan. Chinese everywhere in their blue clothes and their mules, just like Peking! You would enjoy to observe the people of the hills, black-turbaned Shans, Ketchim women in broad 'decolleté,' with a colored kilt, wild Was, almost naked and as shy as jungle animals; a complete ethnological collection."

After a retreat which he spent in 1939 in Peking, he wrote: "I hope to have better focused the aim of my life. In fact, I have the feeling that my life has to be more and more devoted to the discovery (for me and for others) of the wonderful association of universality and personality which is the God we need for being thoroughly human. And I think that for this work of discovery, we are associated." And later that same year from Paris came another letter: "Something deep and broad is obviously moving in the world, and in France specially . . . I have spent hours with the most extraordinary diversity of people . . . and everywhere I find the birth or at least the expectation, of a new creed of man in a spiritual evolution of the world . . . Indeed poor France seems to be tremendously alive inside, much more than any other country in the world. I had the most unexpected meetings with the most influential and, you might say, the most incredulous people in Paris. And each time I realized I could give them, to some extent, the thing they are craving for . . . I am deeply interested in your impressions of Washington. A need of a change in the heart of politics; an *ideal* for democracy; you are absolutely right. I am just having a series of talks on this subject with a group of influential young men in Paris . . . so far as Catholicism and its anti-progressism are concerned . . . well we are changing that in France. If I succeed, something new will come in the world, this is the very fight of my life. Art and Idea . . . I have met the problem already three times since I am in Paris. This is a great question and I need an answer."

"I had one specially interesting talk which will amuse you, to some sixty artists (sculptors,[5] painters, writers, musicians) forming a new section in the group for the study and improvement of man, organized by the French ingénieur Coutrot (in association with Aldous Huxley). I had to address this selected crowd at the end of lunch and my subject was, 'How to understand and use Art in the line of Human energy'—I expressed the idea that art was the expression of the 'exuberance' of human energy, so that its function was to give a kind of consistency, an intuitive and almost instinctive shape, and a *personal* character to this ever growing supply and excess of spiritual forces gradually freed from material ties: just like science and philosophy, but in a much more spontaneous and personalistic way."

That same year, 1939, he had been speaking before some Catholic Clubs for young people, and observed: "I am convinced that we are unconsciously witnessing one of the most startling human movements in history, with *no trace* of hardness nor hatred whatsoever in its progression. Simply love—but love based on the faith that the world is converging into *Somebody,* also loving and definite. And this is the point where my poor intellectual efforts come in: because to these working boys and girls (as well as for other classes of people) my 'views' supply a perspective where the past, the present, and the future meet in an atmosphere of material progress and progressing love. Once more, maybe, a new life is expanding from the masses, below."

What a busy time Père Teilhard had had that year, talking, writing, and seeing so many people of all kinds. He returned to Peking in the autumn of 1939 and was there most of the next few years. As I was also living in Peking, there are few notes or letters, only hours of talk and discussion to remember, but nothing in his exact words to quote. However, a few lines from a Paris letter of 1949 may be of interest as they express the core of so much of his think-

---

[5] This reminds me that perhaps I should add that Père Teilhard was always interested in whatever sculpture I was working on in my studio—whether in Peking or New York. He would look at things a long time and from all angles and then invariably put his finger on the weak spot. He had a great appreciation of Western art and his Western interests were all-encompassing. Even *The New Yorker* was a source of amusement and delight to him—though I often found that trying to explain the very American jokes to a very French Frenchman was beyond my powers!

ing: "My present effort is more and more concentrating on a better analysis of the 'ultra-humain' (existence, nature, and growth): right at this point, I am convinced, hides the source of every modern conflict and hope, because such an *ultra-humain* cannot be accepted (under pressure of facts) without accepting, *ipso facto,* a definite view of the true relationship between spirit and matter, and also a definite 'faith' in the future of man." And a few months later (in 1950) he continued: "My ideas seem to have reached a stage where they grow simpler, fewer and bigger, rather than multiplying. Presently, two points are practically absorbing the whole of my internal attention; the first being that, religiously speaking, the major event in our world is a certain change in 'the face of God' (God becoming a loving Center of universal evolution, rather than the big 'landowner' of yesterday)—and the second being the vital urgence to watch and feed in man *le Goût de vivre* (that is the evolution pressure), which is decidedly the most fundamental of the cosmic energies." And finally in that same year, he wrote: "We are living in a quickly and dangerously moving world. We had better face it— and chiefly to develop a strong faith (based on a clear vision of things) in the future of man."

6

Orthodoxy and Science

By Canon Charles E. Raven

Some fifty years ago a young don from Oxford and a still younger don from Cambridge meeting for the first time at Swanwick spent a long afternoon discussing the impact of a thoroughgoing acceptance of evolution upon Christian theology. They felt that this was a matter with which their generation could not but be vitally concerned. Hitherto, Christians had regarded this world and indeed the universe as of religious importance only because it was the theater in which the drama of man's redemption had been staged. Natural religion was treated as largely irrelevant; indeed Christianity being concerned with the spiritual and eternal was scarcely affected by theories of the origin and character of its temporal prison house. The three centuries of the New Philosophy and of applied science had seen an increasing divorce between the cosmology, geology, biology, and psychology of the modern world and of the Christian tradition; and in 1910 the two were in open collision. It was, as both young men knew, very hard for an honest and intelligent person to be both orthodox and scientific. To realize that the theater and all that it involved was an integral and basic part of the drama was a good starting point for a radical and necessarily universal reinterpretation of experience. They had small knowledge then of the extent and demands of the task before them.

It remained inescapable; and in fact both of them in their different ways made it a chief objective of their working lives. It is the pact of that necessity (which had been realized by many before them and by most thinking people since) that explains the intense interest which the work and works of Father Pierre Teilhard de Chardin have aroused. He more than any other "speaks to our condition."

The publication of his religious masterpiece, *Le Milieu Divin*, in English and the translation of the monumental record of his Life and Thought by Claude Cuénot,[1] following upon that of *The Phenomenon of Man* introduced by Sir Julian Huxley in 1959, give us in the English-speaking world the opportunity for a full appreciation of his meaning and quality, for correcting some of our first impressions, and for realizing his special importance for our own tradition in theology.

The fuller material, and we may add his essay called *La Messe sur le Monde* (the first and in some respects most revealing of his writings) as well as the first two pieces in this book, give us the whole man and disclose the unique integrity of his approach to his whole environment. We have become so obsessed with the belief that religion and science belong to different, and indeed contradictory, elements in experience that a man like Teilhard for whom they are demonstrably one and to be studied by precisely similar methods of observation and testing is inevitably unfamiliar. It is noticeable that even Sir Julian, his friend and admirer who has so strongly commended his work, can only speak of the religion which in fact is inseparable from it as a "gallant attempt to reconcile the supernatural elements in Christianity with the facts and implications of evolution" (*The Phenomenon*, pp. 19 and 22).

It is, of course, fundamental for us to realize that for Teilhard both as human being and as philosopher there is no question of living in two worlds. His experience of life, as is the case with most of us, is of a reaction to the universe in which wonder and awe, a paradoxical sense of unity and solitariness, are combined with intellectual curiosity and practical experiment. Great scientists, as

---

[1] Cuénot, Claude, *Pierre Teilhard de Chardin—les grandes étapes de son évolution* (Paris: Librairie Plon, 1958). The translation, published in United States by Helicon Press, Inc. (Baltimore), will appear sometime in 1964.

the latest interpreter of Charles Darwin, Dr. Loren Eisley, has so explicitly insisted, have combined an aesthetic and religious response to nature with a passionate inquisitiveness of research, and even the pure mathematician, most abstract of them all, speaks of his results in the language of art and beauty. Indeed most of our errors, at least according to the ancient Greeks, arise when our intellectual calculating machines lose touch with the wholeness of our apprehension and so cease to interpret it truthfully. Teilhard was first and last a Christian; he was also a great paleontologist with a keen and wide-ranging mind; and the experience and discipline of his religion entered into and helped to explain his whole scientific and social outlook. So he can use the form and imagery of the Mass to present to God the full extent of the natural order, its diversity and unity, its life and death, its movement and its rest, its beauty and its pain, from the fire of which it is born to the Christ in whom it is fulfilled. And to those of us to whom such rhythm is unfamiliar, it may be good to remember that the greatest of all French naturalists, Jean Henri Fabre, hard-boiled skeptic and "Homer of the insects," when asked about the ghoulish death-role of Nature, declared that the more he studied it the more he was convinced that "all life, however unconsciously, was obedient to a sublime law of sacrifice." It is something of an irony that the religion for which Incarnation, the unity of Godhead and manhood, is central should have accepted, and it must be admitted too often fostered, the error of segregating revelation from nature and Creation from Redemption. Here at least is a man for whom the two are one.

It is unnecessary, for the purpose of this appreciation, to set out in any detail his account of the evolution of the universe as we human beings are now able to experience it. He has seen and studied the whole realm of our cosmic environment, bringing under scrutiny all the data within our apprehension from the radiant energy of its primary "stuff" through the increasing complexities of atomic structure, the convergence of atoms into molecules, the origin of cell formation, the progress from cell to organism, and so to the genealogical tree of vegetable and animal life. He has his own language both for the levels and for the relationships, and this is not always easy to translate: but his picture is universal and coherent, the constantly repeated story of the formation of what Lloyd

Morgan used to call new "fellowships" or symbioses, and the consequent emergence of fresh spheres of being. So he comes to the level of the noosphere, of conscious mental and spiritual life, of "hominization" and the human understanding and control of the evolutionary process, the level for which his own special studies in China and Java and South Africa have made him an outstanding authority. His travels and explorations, his objectivity and his genius for teamwork, his insight in interpreting and his judgment in presenting the verdict upon the data give a vivid impression of his scientific eminence and of his scrupulous fairness. His enthusiasm is always under control, his imagination always attested by the evidence. So when he proceeds from *Sinanthropus* to modern man he is giving us an increasingly rich account of human capabilities and achievements, individual and collective, secular and religious. He is not, as Dr. Cuénot admits, a trained historian and does not attempt to cover the whole story of civilization, but he insists, as everyone who takes evolution seriously must do, that the character of the process is to be estimated not by its origins but by its whole present attainments and future possibilities. So he does not hesitate to insist upon what he calls the "unanimization" of the human world-wide community and looks forward to its "Christification" at the point of consummation, the Omega of the record. Perhaps his very remarkable visualizing of Christ in the extract about the painting from *Le Cœur de la Matière* (first essay in this book) is a description of the final world-culminating Omega.

In all this Teilhard is careful to insist that he is concerned with phenomena not with metaphysics, and on points upon which he must inevitably differ from the tradition is not only scrupulously careful to admit the fact but does so with complete modesty and gentleness. Nevertheless, in his findings reached with objectivity and sincerity, he is in fact calling us not to a novelty but to the great succession, the earliest and most authentic Christian doctrine; to the religious mysticism of the prologue to the Fourth Gospel and the progressive interpretation of the significance of Christ in the epistles of Saint Paul; to the Logos-theology of the Greek Apologists, to Irenaeus and Athanasius who said of Jesus that "he became human in order that we might become divine"; to the Christian philosophy of Clement and Origen with its universalism, its sense of progress and coherence, its scholarship and its insight, and to the recurrent and for us today inescapable appeal of Christian Platonism. It is the theology that was restated in Britain in the seventeenth century by Joseph Mead, Benjamin Whichcote, and Ralph Cudworth and was accepted by Christians as different as John Tillotson, Richard Baxter, and the early Quakers, and that created a climate of opinion wholly favorable to the study of nature and so contributed immensely to the success of the Royal Society and the establishment and prestige of science in England. Incidentally, Cudworth's theory of "plastic nature" and of the status of man has much in common with Teilhard's own philosophy.

The value of this succession is a matter of high theological importance. To very many of us in these years of distress and of opportunity the stature and significance of Saint Paul have been the great discovery—that he was not in his true self the teacher so sadly caricatured because of his references to "the powers that be," or to predestination, or to the subjugation of woman, or to a crude eschatology, but the seer who step by step perceived and proclaimed the majesty, the efficacy, and the universality of Christ. In reality he, even more concretely than Saint John, disclosed the true nature of God as love; of love as not only the means of our individual transformation but the nexus of the world-wide community; of Christ as the embodiment and actualizing of the true life of a world whose whole nature revealed and whose whole history affirmed his "many-colored splendor." We, like Teilhard, had fastened upon the apostle's culminating vision in Philippians, Colossians, and Ephesians of a single superhuman organism in which mankind found its fulfillment. We were discovering evidence of its appropriateness and inspiration to its service from the contemporary crises of events and the discoveries of recent science. For us Teilhard consolidates, unifies, and expresses our faith, with a completeness and a consistency which are abundantly compelling.

This expression, as he explains it and we have sought it, is a study of universal phenomena. Nevertheless, such phenomena so interpreted constitute a theology. Here is a doctrine of the Godhead in relation to the "cosmogenesis," the creative, redemptive, sanctifying process, in which the whole noosphere is involved and "hominization" and "divinization" are successive stages: a doctrine which transcends our familiar dualisms, and resolves the paradoxes of matter and spirit, individual and community, good and evil. We can reformulate our Christology in terms of Christ the *pleroma;* can work out a new theory of Atonement centered on the concept of *Christus Consummator,* a phrase used by Teilhard himself; can discover at last a satisfying faith in the Spirit, the Holy One, as we realize that from the primal energy onward the universe is capable of and responds to the emergence of new relationships, at once "complexified" and "converging." This will give us an orthodoxy emancipated from the categories of pre-Christian, pre-Copernican or pre-Darwinian cosmologies and expressed in terms that illuminate the intellectual and moral, the active and passive, the "tangential" and the "radical" energies of mankind, an orthodoxy arrived at by strictly scientific methods and capable of rallying humanity to the "universalism," "futurism," and "personalism" of his little war book *Sauvons L'humanité* distributed in 1940 to a few officers of the French Army.[2]

It is perhaps easier for an Englishman to appreciate the substantial orthodoxy of Teilhard than for his own compatriots. Dr. Cuénot's biography, immensely rich in its quotations from his own letters and unpublished writings and thoroughly exact in its mass of detail, gives us very little information as to the forerunners of his great synthesis or of the influence upon him of his teachers and church. Apparently though he inherited a love of nature and of the earth, of Christ and of God, he was brought up on traditional lines, as a *fixiste* in regard to creation, and even in geology, his first subject of study, was not deeply concerned with the origin of species until his discovery of Bergson's *Creative Evolution.* Evolution which had until then been a nineteenth-century theory became a fascinating and dominant conviction; M. Boule of the Musée, E. Le Roy of the College, M. Blondel, the philosopher, and later in life Lucien Cuénot, the biologist, and above all the Abbé Breuil were his friends: during the war when he served as a stretcher bearer, during the whole period he came to appreciate both the facts on which "transformism" was based and the evidence which testified to its influence upon progress. Unfortunately no one, so far as we know,

[2] Cf. Cuénot, pp. 267-8 in French edition.

has given us a detailed record of the sources of his philosophy; and his own references make it probable that he had arrived at his basic sense of the wholeness, continuity, and direction of the creative process largely by direct study and thought. No doubt Maurice Blondel and others of his friends contributed; and Bergson must have been to him as to most of us in those days an excitement and provocation. But he seems never to have accepted the idea of an *élan vital* acting upon and subjugating matter or the antithesis between instinct and intellect. His sense of the continuity of evolution and the concomitance in it, even at the atomic level, of physical and psychic potentialities gave him a wider concept of a universal movement than most of us have even now accepted.

It would be tempting to hope that he learned much from his boyhood exile to Jersey and afterward his four years at Ore near Hastings where he studied theology and did some work on the geology and botany of the Weald. But there is in fact no evidence of contact with the sort of inquiries into evolution that were prominent at that time; and his friendship with Dr. George B. Barbour and a few other British scientists only began after his settlement in China. Even then he never seems to have been aware of the succession of British philosophers and biologists who produced work so like his own in the 1920's, of Samuel Alexander, C. Lloyd Morgan, A. N. Whitehead, Field Marshal Jan C. Smuts, and the Scots, Thompson of Aberdeen, Simpson of Edinburgh and others, or with the theologians B. H. Streeter and W. R. Inge, John Oman and William Temple who made us confident that a revival of the Platonist tradition and an evolutionary scheme which allowed, as A. S. Pringle-Pattison had put it, both for continuity of process and for the emergence of novelty, would give us a reasonable and relevant restatement.

Indeed before the influence of this group had made itself felt the blight which infected our theology with the spread of transcendentalism and its rejection of natural religion, the assertion of biblical authoritarianism and neo-orthodoxy, and the pessimism created by the fear of a second world war, had emptied religion of hope, confined faith to narrow limits, and treated liberalism as synonymous with apostasy. It is notable that according to Dr. Cuénot when after his return to France Teilhard settled, under coercion, in America and met Anglo-Saxon scientists he found them notably learned but embedded in their scientism, positivism and neo-Darwinism; "with few exceptions they are incapable of following philosophic thought" (Cuénot, p. 198). This verdict he had no real chance of revising—though apparently he found it a stimulant.

This is indeed one of the tragic consequences of the decision of his superiors and of the Vatican that he must not publish any of his books during his lifetime. Though he had long ago established a great reputation as a paleontologist, geologist, and authority upon human origins, his exposition of his larger views was thereby confined to articles in the scientific press, to addresses at specialist conferences, and at occasional and semiprivate lectures. A few of his writings were circulated to friends in cyclostyled copies, but even *La Messe, Le Milieu* and *Le Phénomène*, which he regarded as the most important and which he submitted to the authorities several times in amended forms, were almost unknown. Even those of us who were working on his lines and in fields close to his own hardly knew his name. This man who held a message for the Church and the world intensely valuable and relevant was allowed to die in virtual exile, almost alone, and with no certainty that his work would ever be recognized or allowed to be submitted to readers.

The courage, the self-effacement, the friendliness with which he faced isolation and frustration, and resisted every suggestion that he should follow the way of Renan and Loisy and refuse to be silenced, are set out with a fine restraint and a complete absence of bitterness by his friends and biographer. But all who realize the outstanding quality and gifts of the man and who would have gained immeasurably by study and examination of his works, and have furnished him with opportunities for expounding the range and wisdom of his convictions and for sharing the inspiration of his vision, will regard the loss to the world in its years of agony as irreparable.

For his greatness consists not only in the fact that he has formulated an interpretation of our world unique in its scale and integrity, a philosophy profoundly impressive at once in its range of knowledge, its consistency of outlook, and its practicality and concreteness, but has worked out the application of his system of thought so as to relate it not only to the problems of individual behavior but to the crucial and world-wide issues of socialization and the building up of human community. Here is a man in mind as in character "all of a piece," with the love of God as the point of convergence for his whole person. Hence he gives an impression both of full maturity and of unity in multiplicity. His actions and opinions carry weight because they express in each particular the application of an identical standard and the statement of an inevitable conclusion. A few instances chosen almost at random from the wide variety of his interests will illustrate.

Take first his central conviction in the crucial matter of the tension between inward constraint and outward association. He writes, "Is it not a fact, as I can warrant, that if the love of God was extinguished in the souls of the faithful, the enormous edifice of rites, of hierarchy, and of doctrines that comprise the Church would instantly revert to the dust from which it rose?" (*The Phenomenon,* pp. 295-6) and again, "What is most divine in God is that, in an absolute sense, we are nothing apart from him. The least admixture of what may be called Pelagianism would suffice to ruin immediately the beauties of the divine *milieu* in the eyes of the seer" (*Milieu,* p. 17). And of the resulting universalism he writes, "Within the Church we observe all sorts of groups whose members are vowed, to the perfect practice of this or that particular virtue, mercy, detachment, the splendor of the liturgy, the missions, contemplation. Why should there not be men vowed to the task of exemplifying by their lives the general sanctification of human endeavor" (*Milieu,* p. 39). So of his own conflict of loyalties when the refusal to allow publication of his books constrained his friends to counsel resistance, "I should believe myself guilty of betraying the 'World' if I withdrew from the position assigned to me in it. . . . The Society is not less but more and more precisely *my* point of insertion and of work in the Universe" (Cuénot, p. 149, quoting letters of June and September, 1929).

In other fields here is his reaction to Dr. Oakley's exposure of the Piltdown skull, with which he had been concerned when he met Dawson in his younger days and of which he had always been suspicious. "Anatomically speaking, Eoanthropus was a sort of monster; paleontologically it was a shock that at the dawn of humanity a man could appear in England. So I am fundamentally satisfied by your conclusions although sentimentally speaking I make a mess of one of my earliest memories" (Cuénot, p. 37, quoting letter of November, 1953). And of a theological error more recent and dangerous, the denial in some Christian circles that there can be any real progress by mankind or any perfecting of this world: "If progress is a myth, that is to say, if faced by the work involved we can say 'What's the good of it all?' our efforts will flag. With that the whole of evolution will come to a halt—because we are evolution. All conscious energy is, like love (and because it is love), founded on hope" (*The Phenomenon*, p. 233). And finally of one of his most speculative propositions, the development of one soul in the integrated community: "The idea that some Soul of souls should be developing at the summit of the world is not as strange as might be thought from the present day views of human reason. After all, is there any other way in which our thought can generalize the Principle of Emergence?" (*The Phenomenon*, pp. 268-9, with note citing J. B. S. Haldane's *Inequality of Man*, p. 113) and similarly, "The only subject ultimately capable of mystical transfiguration is the whole group of mankind forming a single body and a single soul in charity" (*Milieu*, p. 138).

Postscript, 1964

It is with some hesitation that I have agreed to the reissue of this essay here in its original form. It was written originally at a time when several volumes of Teilhard's letters and papers were not yet in print and the spate of comment on him, that is now about us, had hardly begun. For me, my book *Teilhard de Chardin: Scientist and Seer* (London: Collins, 1962; New York: Harper) "dates" this essay. Yet to rewrite it would involve a repetition of what is already in circulation. So the essay's value, if any, is that of a preliminary verdict, a verdict which has been strongly confirmed not least by Teilhard's most hostile critic Professor P. B. Medawar, whose recent Herbert Spencer Lecture (1963) puts forward as his own a view of evolution as threefold, "chemical, organic, and psychosocial," the identical interpretation explored by Teilhard and E. Le Roy in their theory of hydrosphere, biosphere, and noosphere in 1925 and published in full detail by Le Roy in his *Essai d'une Philosophie Première* (pp. 330-422) with recognition of Teilhard's share in responsibility for it, and by Teilhard in *The Phenomenon of Man* and elsewhere.

7

Teilhard's Achievement

By D. M. MacKinnon

The future may well see the great achievement of Teilhard to lie (his technical articles apart) in the field of spirituality. For although *Le Milieu Divin* was written before *Le Phénomène Humain,* and can indeed probably be taken as an introduction to the elusive arcana of the latter work, it seems to me incomparably the greater, and to be an achieved masterpiece which, if in the first instance a spiritual treatise, is also profoundly suggestive for the constructive philosopher and theologian.

It is clear there is a characteristically Anglo-Saxon distaste for essays in *Naturphilosophie.* I say a characteristically Anglo-Saxon distaste, for such essays in this field as those of A. N. Whitehead's later period, and of Samuel Alexander, tend to be regarded by those who stand within the historic tradition of British empiricism as aberrations of mind on the part of their authors. (I am told that the same situation largely holds in America.) There is of course one exception to this rule in the late R. G. Collingwood's *Idea of Nature,* which was posthumously published in 1945 (although I heard the substance of the greater part of it delivered as lectures in Oxford in 1934); and while it is true both that Collingwood's work was tragically cut short by illness and death, and that his writings are very largely, although by no means entirely, neglected today (he does not rate a mention in Geoffrey Warnock's book on the history of British philosophy in this century in the *Home University Library*), he remains a most formidable figure, whose capacity for asking awkward questions must comprise a powerful irritant in the minds of any who bother to read his works. Collingwood did take *Naturphilosophie* seriously; and if the bias of philosophy of science is avowedly, and quite properly, methodological in preoccupation, no one who has read Collingwood's book or its companion *Essay on Metaphysics* (published in 1940), can ever be quite sure that neglect of *Naturphilosophie* is always a mark of disciplined, intellectual discrimination.

There is of course the further and crucial question of the sort of insight that *Naturphilosophie* may confer, and the manner in which these insights are to be received. Where Teilhard's disputed *Le Phénomèné Humain* is concerned, Dr. Paul Cauchard in his *L'Être Humain selon Teilhard de Chardin* has stressed the importance of a proper understanding of what Teilhard conceived phenomenology to be; and this work among the voluminous French output on its subject seems to me (apart from Cuénot's biography) the most helpful. In any appraisal of the book *Le Phénomène Humain,* an exact appreciation of how its author conceived his own essay on philosophy of nature is certainly desirable; and it must be admitted that the ambiguity on the Continent of the term phenomenology, which is the term he uses to designate the scope and limitation of his own enterprise, but uses in his own special sense, contributes to obscurity here.

But where *Le Milieu Divin* is concerned, we have a sketch of the author's image of the world presented as the fruit of an interrogative meditation, in which the reader is invited to join. *Naturphilosophie* is in some sense a kind of metaphysics; I say in some sense, for Teilhard himself differentiates metaphysics (conceived as ontology) from the sort of phenomenology he offers. It lies therefore under the many forms of ban imposed, thanks to the devoted and successful efforts of critical philosophers, upon what we call metaphysics. Thus his use of the term *evolution* (a term that has suffered much in the last century at the hands of those who have sought to make it an instrument of a comprehensive and universal wisdom) lays him open at once to the sharp comment of those who have learned from Kant, to notice quickly the metaphysician's illicit transition from the relative to the absolute use of a concept. But in *Le Milieu Divin* we have *Naturphilosophie* presented to us as something we are to make our own in a context of prayer and meditation. If as Wittgenstein suggests, it is "in the stream of life that an expression has meaning," we may well claim that it is in the movement of our reflective devotion that the language of *Le Milieu Divin* has its sense. So the idiom of *Naturphilosophie,* however vulnerable to the critical philosopher, finds its home in religious exercise; metaphysical idiom is consciously bedded down again in the religious life in which it takes its origin. But if this is in one sense, for metaphysics, a loss of the kind of autonomy which men sought to gain for it when presenting it as a set of rationally defensible, unconditionally valid truths concerning the nature of what is, in another sense the insertion of such highly self-conscious reflection concerning the universe around us into religious meditation bestows upon the latter a quality of intellectual rigor and seriousness that it very easily loses, that it has indeed lost, and is continually in threat of losing.

Devotion is incurably anthropocentric; and this is true even when the devout man has purged out of his imagination the corrupting influence of anthropomorphism, and (more technically) pursues the road of a theocentric as distinct from a Christocentric spirituality. Whether prayer be public or private, liturgical or extempore, it is still human prayer, and by that very fact suffused with the praying subject's sense that his concerns, and those of the human race to which he belongs, are of overwhelming significance to the one whom he addresses. If in defense of this attitude, he pleads a greater value to reside in a man than in many sparrows, or echoes Pascal's often quoted words concerning the "thinking reed," his argument may sometimes quiet his uncertainty, but only perhaps for a while. To pray demands of a man that he supposes himself and his Lord the center of the world, and that he pays more than lip service to the insistence of such men as Augustine and Newman, that two things above all are luminously evident, God and the human soul.

If religious men are honest with themselves, they are aware of a malaise as they become self-conscious of the hardly curable anthropocentrism of their religious attitudes. Moreover, if for a moment we turn aside from religion to the territory of critical philosophy, we cannot help being struck with analogous disquiet. There is no doubt whatsoever of the growing hold on educated opinion of ideas, which would treat the fundamental explanatory concepts of the exact sciences, with their clearly defined functions in explanatory hypotheses, as in some sense, human inventions. Such a view is perfectly compatible with attaching extreme importance to the role of induction, in the sense of bold generalization from collocations of observed fact, in the sciences; it is much more a doctrine concerning the nature of certain sorts of fundamental concepts. Similarly in the philosophy of mathematics itself, a central debate concerns the question how far a new piece of mathematics is properly regarded as other than a free invention or spontaneous creation. But such views inevitably provoke an answering disquiet, which I can only characterize as realist. Is there no such thing as mathematical discovery? Do not the characteristic outlooks of such sciences as geology and biology set a question mark against any view which tends, however rigorously the tendency is mitigated by a precise logical analysis of the nature of conceptual thinking, in the direction of a modified subjectivism, using the term to indicate a doctrine which treats fundamental explanatory concepts as constructions or inventions? No doubt this malaise is curable by critical philosophical work; but its occurrence bears witness to our hard-won bias toward some kind of realism, a bias that refuses us to allow a model of the world we recognize to be made after our own image, to be regarded as a last word concerning the way we receive what we assert of that world.

Now Teilhard's meditation is supremely relevant here. He catches and transforms, into the stuff of reflective prayer, the dialogue within a man himself that I have here illustrated. If philosophical disputes require to be worked out, so do the religious, metaphysical disquiets which issue from our sense, for instance, of the scale of the universe, of the circumstances of the origin of human life. P. B. Medawar in his very valuable collection of essays, *The Uniqueness of the Individual* (1957), has written illuminatingly on the imperfections of men (pp. 122f.). No student of the philosophy of religion can fail to see the bearing of his careful description of the actualities of our human state on the structure so massively and impressively built by the late F. R. Tennant in the second volume of his *Philosophical Theology* (1930). Tennant's statement of the "argument from design" in his chapter in that volume on cosmic teleology is masterly; but his viewpoint is *malgré lui-même* incurably anthropocentric. He does not achieve that cool, analytical detachment, which Medawar, in his list of human imperfections, has certainly reached. This, although unlike the overtly anthropocentric modern theologians of the school of Rudolf Bultmann, Tennant hoped he had escaped by his long previous discussions, the bondage of an introspective preoccupation with our characteristically human attitudes!

What Teilhard does *inter multa alia* is to present, as a most necessary spiritual and intellectual exercise, the setting of a question mark against our assumption that the world is run for our benefit. He suggests that the dimension of a cosmic awareness must be restored to Christian existence at the level of prayer and of thought. In fact by the example of his book, he shows how both restorations can and must be carried out together. To say this is not to forget the serious inadequacies we can discern in his treatment of evil, and of the discontinuities in natural and human existence, nor the great necessity of complementing his image by others as powerful; it is only to advertise the liberating force of his work in an age when religious thinkers are not infrequently tempted to escape the fundamental malaise, springing from their dim perception of the anthropocentrism of their theology, by making a virtue of that failure and converting faith into a special sort of self-knowledge, thus deepening the troubles they should seek to cure.

Medawar in a highly critical notice in *Mind* (January, 1961) of *The Phenomenon of Man* refers to Teilhard's "moderate competence" in a branch of science, viz. paleontology, moderate in its demand of vigorous exactitude. It is not for me to appraise Teilhard's paleontological work; but it is arguable (and here perhaps I betray the continuing influence on me of some of Collingwood's ideas) that only a man, practicing a science forcing him to be aware of the history of the universe, could have achieved the kind of self-consciousness Teilhard won his way to. We are familiar enough with philosophical work on the nature of scientific explanation, the status of natural laws, and the import of fundamental explanatory concepts which encourage us to discern in the achievement of natural and exact scientists (different in many particulars though the methods of the observational and experimental sciences may be) something that bears written upon it the hallmark of a human victory over our natural environment. Such views can be traced in writers as various as those who seek to make good the deficiencies of the so-called "descriptive theory of science" associated with the name of Ernst Mach (e.g. A. J. Ayer), and John MacMurray who, in his illuminating Gifford lectures on *The Form of the Personal* (Vol. I, 1957: Vol II, 1961), has argued strongly that what we are doing in seeking to understand our world, can only itself be understood when we take the revolutionary step of recognizing both the primacy of the practical and also the necessarily social character of that human situation which all the time is eliciting practical response from us. But Teilhard's sense of the reaches of the past, and indeed of the future, inevitable even in a moderately competent paleontologist but only brought to deep self-consciousness in such a one as Teilhard himself, prevents him from resting in such relatively consoling positions; for so at times these positions must appear. He knows that men must view their setting from another perspective, and complement such images of their human task by others; and this he realizes is at once intellectually and spiritually binding on those who would be delivered from the bondage of a cosmos and a creator fashioned after the imagined needs of their souls.

His way is not the only way; and this he recognizes, suggesting indeed in modesty that the true metaphysician has penetrated the deeps of the relation of becoming to being *hic et nunc* in a manner impossible to one essaying the elaborate and often (let us admit) confused exposé of the phenomenology (in his sense) of the world. But in *Le Milieu Divin* he provides the context within which such phenomenology, however inaccurate and tendentious in detail, may be received as liberation: as liberation indeed in a task of very great difficulty, that of bringing together the supposed finalities of Christian faith with the recognition that men, to learn what they are, must divest themselves of the illusion that the secret of what is, is something which they can read off from themselves, constraining the world, however diverse the methods of constraint, to an image of their own devising.

Where Christology is concerned, in however incomplete a form, Teilhard offers a new form of the doctrine of the "cosmic Christ." Nicholas Corte's comparison of his work with Origen's is suggestive;

it would also be fascinating to trace, in some of his pages, the presence of ideas of *recapitulatio* akin to those found in Irenaeus. No one who reads *Le Milieu Divin* carefully can doubt that his Ignatian exercises have well schooled the author in sensitive awareness of the perpetual simplicities of the Christian way. Yet all who read the same pages must surely welcome the boldness with which, for all his concern with the interior life, he refuses to subdue the idea of the cosmic role of the Lord Jesus to the level of a mythological transcript of the never diminished, effective, spiritual sovereignty of the one who evokes the response of faith. If he leaves the doctrine of the "cosmic Christ" as something restored to the status of a grave and pressing problem, he has further put Christian thought in his debt. That the Christian faith may fail to measure up to the needs and perspectives of a new age is a possibility that any Christian, who is serious about the involvement of his faith in the relativities of history and his consequent inescapable commitment to the affirming of finality in a life that had its place and its time, must surely acknowledge. Because it is a characteristic and inescapable obligation of Christian faith to "run risk" in the response to new perspectives, we are deeply in Teilhard's debt for his delineation of some of the most characteristic modern risks which he has not himself hesitated to face.

8

Saint Augustine and Teilhard

By Karl Stern

The student of evolution works like a detective. He collects his pieces of evidence on a world-wide scale, a jawbone here, a tibia there. A fossil appears, fixed in rock like a cosmic fingerprint; a fish who was believed extinct is taken alive from the sea, like a star witness who had been presumed dead. But quite contrary to the common detective story, the more the fragments of evidence *fit* the more our detective must refrain from looking for a perpetrator. The scientific theory of evolution is like a thriller without a whodunit. The sleuth must trace everything back but never to a culprit (this would betray a metaphysical bias), and he must introduce all working assumptions except a motive (this would amount to a teleological bias).

The scientists who impose such frustrating and paradoxical rules are justified up to a point. Here, as we shall presumably see, the aim transcends the method—a special case in that detective story which we call scientific discovery. There are other reasons for which the rules of the game have to be strict. The theoretician of evolution is related to the ordinary biologist as a philosopher of history is to a historian; as Toynbee or Sorokin or Spengler are to Ranke or Mommsen or Trevelyan. Now there exists a deep distrust of the specialist toward the man with the unifying approach. This distrust is not always objective; it often contains a hidden human element. Some of the critics of Arnold Toynbee among his fellow historians have been more passionate than the occasion would warrant, and one is justified in suspecting a personal resentment. And part of it is this: scientific research implies an attitude of mental asceticism. It is much more fun to indulge in the philosophy of nature than to do a decent bit of experimental research. It is more fun to speculate about the meaning of history than to assemble data. Therefore those who spend their lives as humble diggers resent the sweeping gesture coming from the direction of an armchair. Incidentally, it seems that those who are the more fortunate in the "sweep" are frequently men who themselves have gone through a long apprenticeship in the patient groundwork of science.

Thoughts like these occurred to me on reading Teilhard de Chardin's work, and the controversial literature concerning him. It is always fascinating to look at a scientist *sub specie temporis,* i.e., within the setting of a certain phase of history. The fact that the *Zeitgeist* expresses itself similarly in divergent fields of human activity appears understandable when we remain confined to the aesthetic. It appears more difficult to accept the conclusion that science, too, should be part of the same historical process. We think we can see why Picasso, Joyce, and Stravinsky were contemporaries and did, in three quite different fields, things which are strangely comparable. But the fact that Newton "belongs" with Bach is more puzzling, and more suggestive of coincidence and idle speculation. The reason is probably that we are inclined to underestimate the objective element in the aesthetic creation, and the subjective element in the scientific discovery.

When we look from this point of view at the theory of evolution we see that, quite independently from the question of its truth or untruth, it "belongs" to the nineteenth century. However, the reasons are strangely contrasting. The beginning of the industrial revolution was associated with an extraordinary emphasis on progress. Thus, it is not at all surprising to see that the concept of an advance by improved production should have inspired biologists. The idea that in the vast workshop of nature things which do not work so well should be discarded in favor of things which work better arises quite understandably out of the mood of the time. However, that faith in progress belongs at the same time to quite another modality. To nineteenth-century thinkers human history was a *process of unfolding*. The Christian eschatological idea of history, as a temporal series with an immanent and transcendental goal, which had gone underground long before, now lifted its head, strangely disguised, in the world of Herder and Hegel, Marx and Nietzsche.

These two aspects of progress, the one of mechanics and the one of historicity, have both entered into the theory of evolution to varying degrees at various times. Before we go further into this we must first make another distinction. We encounter the theory of evolution under several aspects. There is a working hypothesis for the use of the biologist which serves to explain otherwise puzzling phenomena—such as the geographical distribution of plants and animals, the extinction of certain species and the survival of others. This was the theory which Darwin on the *Beagle* originally developed. Such a theory has no philosophical implications, and it is hard to see how anyone who is not a well-trained biologist can venture to quarrel with it. But then there exists that other *global* aspect to the theory of evolution. Here the theory answers questions about creation, and the nature and destiny of man, his being and his becoming, and his position in the universe around him. In most cases this theory attempts to replace religious concepts by something which is "closer to truth." We are told that in the atheistic museums of the Soviet Union the story of the universe is presented pictorially for the enlightenment of the onlooker, to demonstrate that scientific research has done away with religious notions which are held to be manifestations of archaic and superstitious thinking. The same is true about a great deal of the literature of evolution since Thomas Huxley and Ernst Haeckel. Let us, for the sake of argument, present this global concept of evolution in a radically positivist formulation. Then we would have to say something like this: at a certain moment in time the temperature of the earth was such that it became most favorable for the aggregation of carbon atoms, and of nitrogen with hydrogen, and for the carbon atoms and the oxygen to combine with the nitrogen and hydrogen and that from random clusters certain molecules occurred which were most favorably structured for the coming-about of life, and from that it went on through vast stretches of time until by advancing natural selection, a being finally occurred which is capable of choosing love over hatred, justice over injustice, writing poetry like that of Dante, composing music like that of Mozart and making drawings like those of Leonardo. Of course, such a view of cosmogenesis is crazy. And I do not at all mean crazy in the sense of slangy invective but rather in the technical meaning of psychotic. Indeed, such a view of the history of the world has a lot in common with certain aspects of schizophrenic thinking. I shall not pursue this idea any further here.[1]

The only important thing in this connection is to see *why* such a view of cosmogenesis is absurd. And the very first and most obvious objection is that no degree of development and structurization of matter explains the phenomenon of consciousness. We could, theoretically, build a huge electronic memory machine which stores and "processes" all events in the world from now until some indefinite time, but we could not give it consciousness. (Cybernetics, as de Broglie pointed out, has left the phenomenon of consciousness as mysterious as it was before.)

All materialistic theories of evolution had to make a cautious detour around the problem of consciousness. The reason for this is simple. A theory, to remain strictly scientific, has to treat the world around us, the stars and the nebulae, the rocks and the seas, the trees and herbs, the fishes and the anthropoids, as an object, as some huge, monstrous *res extensa* which I can *analyze* experimentally and mathematically but into which I *cannot enter* intuitively. If I insist on treating the universe around me as such a scientific object I have to assume a strange attitude; I have to cease to *belong* to the universe I am studying. At first sight this seems paradoxical. Are we not told that the "biological [Darwinian] insult," as Freud called it, was so hard to take just because it kicked man from a lofty anthropocentric position right into the animal world, and made him part of the biological series? In reality, the moment we look at something purely scientifically we are alienated from it. We are confronted with it as with a reaction in a test tube. The cosmos we look at may be infinitely more complex than the process of $Ca\,CO_3$ + $2HCl$ but it is, in principle, still the same. It is an object, a

---

[1] There is so much of the psychological *argumentum ad hominem,* of the clinical name calling in materialistic philosophies, that it would be only too tempting to apply the same method for the opposite argument!

Gegenstand (literally something opposed to me), a matter of mere existence, hopelessly and forever estranged.

Besides such a view of nature as a huge *res extensa* there is another view of, or rather relationship to, nature. Man can grasp nature intuitively, by inner union. This attitude prevailed in rural civilizations, wherever man was imbedded in nature, rather than piercing it with analytical tools. It still prevails in certain Eastern civilizations and philosophies; it prevailed in Europe during the Middle Ages. On the religious plane, at least in the West, it came to its greatest flowering in Franciscan spirituality but it would be quite wrong to regard the attitude we are talking about only as a "religious experience." One thing is true: this relationship cannot be scientifically objectivated. It takes place in what Northrop calls the *aesthetic continuum*. Indeed, ever since the rise of science in our Western civilization this particular relationship to nature has gradually become limited to the artistic and poetic experience.

Such nonscientific relationship to nature presupposes a sense of belonging, a knowledge of intimacy, which the method of scientific inquiry must strictly avoid. Dürer's presentation of a rabbit or a clump of grass conveys a knowledge of nature which no scientific inquiry, on account of its very method, can ever give us. The reason why most of us hesitate to apply the word "knowledge" to the insight within the "aesthetic continuum" and want to reserve it strictly for scientific knowledge is that our minds have become so warped by the positivist bias that we cannot think straight any more. I do not say that one knowledge is more superficial or more profound than the other. But they occur on two different planes. Of course, Dürer's rabbit, no matter how long I contemplate it, will not save me a course in the natural sciences. On the other hand all the thousand observations from the fields of comparative zoology, embryology, cytology, biochemistry which we have accumulated about the phenomenon "rabbit" will never, if added up, amount to the insight which Dürer's rabbit conveys. The aesthetic experience is an immediate experience of essence, a *Wesensschau* in the sense of Husserl. The scientist elucidates an object of nature as it *exists*, the artist elucidates its *being*.

Dionysius the Areopagite and Saint Thomas have used the term connaturality only with reference to human qualities, such as virtues and vices. (I can achieve a knowledge of courage and cowardice in others because I know these qualities from within myself.) Actually there is a form of knowledge by connaturality also with reference to animals and plants. What distinguishes my naïve experience of the rabbit or my experience of Dürer's rabbit from the knowledge gained from a research handbook on the rabbit is an inner participation, a relatedness which is perhaps best described with a term which Max Scheler uses (though in a different connection)—*Kreatürlichkeit* (creatureliness). I am conatured with an animal by my creatureliness. I know perfectly well that in a treatise on evolution this statement means begging the question. But this is just the point. Nothing of the historical order can be understood by the cumulative sciences. To understand the life history of a single individual we need, besides the mosaic of observable facts, our understanding by connaturality. To understand world history the facts accumulated by historians are not enough. We have to add the function of *Einfühlung* (empathy), as Wilhelm Dilthey has pointed out. And now we see that for the historicity of nature, too, a reconstruction of causalities is not enough. Thus there exists a phenomenology of nature which enables us to know a living universe not by analytical penetration and disassembling, not by *Gegenständlichkeit* (objectivation) but by union, by connaturality. This is a universe to which I *belong*. While in the natural sciences the living objects are opaque and denatured by conceptualization (Haas), in the aesthetic continuum they remain translucent and I can interiorize them. To most people the only authentic component in the aesthetic experience is something vaguely emotional.[2]

---

[2] I once participated in a radio debate with a well-known scientist who was a professed atheist. Our subject was "Science and Faith." We came to talk about communication and I ventured the remark that a fugue by Bach contained more truth than quite a few verbalized items in the morning's newspaper. At this my adversary was genuinely amused, and corrected me, stating that a fugue by Bach was a "purely emotional experience" which had nothing to do with truth. We forget only too easily that with the fearful dichotomy of our modern minds the values, aesthetic and moral, become not only arbitrary but also expendable. After a five-course feasting on European civilization we can either retire to the drawing room to discuss serious business or to the *salon* to look at lovely paintings and listen to nocturnes. The aesthetic as a pleasant emotional cloud is a romantic notion, and romanticism was the corollary of the first wave of industrialism.

To the naïve beholder of nature every phenomenon whether it be a lion or a rose, a lizard or a fir tree—conveys a sense of completion in itself. The ensemble of these phenomena conveys a sense of order, even to those who have never heard of ecology or such things. The idea that all these living things are random points of arrestation, as it were, in a blind mechanism of physical occurrences, governed by pragmatic advantages, is difficult to accept. We forget only too easily that the burden of proof is on those who want to impose a mechanistic explanation on phenomena which, to our *Wesensschau,* have the immediate, irreducible quality of createdness.

Let us then summarize by stating that there exist two methods by which we can approach the phenomena of nature: the poetic-intuitive and the scientific-analytic, and that they are of equal validity, each on its own plane, but not of equal applicability. Then we realize that the scientific-analytic method, with all its breath-taking results, cannot possibly be applied to a great number of questions; such as the mystery of creation, the infinite variety of living forms, the destiny of man, the presence of hate and corruption and their coexistence, in the same world, with love and beauty. As is well known, many contemporary positivists go so far as to deny the validity and genuineness of these problems. At any rate, the problems belong to a category which cannot be objectivated; they belong to the *inwardness* of things. There is such an inwardness to the process of becoming. We do not have to go as far as cosmogenesis. I myself have at a certain time been a single cell, microscopically small, and now I sit at a desk, writing. Millions of data from the cumulative sciences form a fearfully intricate net of causalities to tackle this mystery but my being and my becoming are not caught in the meshes of the net. This is equally true about cosmogenesis. The tissue of causalities is still more vast, still more intricately interlaced, truly unsurveyable for any single human being; no matter how many threads one unravels—what one is looking for remains forever elusive. Creation and redemption, if they are true, must be free acts, simple and unique, and millions of causalities do not add up to one free act. This was probably the deeper meaning of Bergson's reaction against the mechanistic concepts of evolution of his time. However, Bergson (at least at the time of *l'Evolution Créatrice*) did not find the solution in the inner historicity of Christian anthropol-

ogy which is experienced intuitively and affirmed mythopoeically.
("Mythopoeic" in this context does not mean "invented and imagi-
nary" and therefore untrue. However, to define the criterion of
truth in the mythopoeic as compared to the scientific in history
would go beyond the scope of this essay.) At any rate, an "inner
anthropology," a concept of man which considers his position within
the hierarchy of living forms, and with this the world of anxiety
and happiness, guilt and atonement, loneliness and acceptance, love
and hatred can never be clarified within a *res extensa,* a sequence of
mechanisms (from water and ammonia to the highest organic structures) which only *explains* the world without comprehending it. It
is clarified only by a historicity (from the Garden of Eden to the
Garden of Gethsemane) which comprehends the world without an
attempt to *explain* it.[3]

Incidentally, this does not mean that the symbols and language
of science cannot be used to hint at things of the inward order. It
has often occurred to me that the doctrine of the Fall, for example,
would be taken seriously by scientists if it were presented as a scientific hypothesis, instead of as a revealed truth. Ortega y Gasset once
remarked, when speaking of biographies: "Every life is, more or less,
a ruin among whose debris we have to discover what the person
ought to have been." One could say the same thing about the history of nature. That strange juxtaposition of harmony and perfection on one hand, and of spoiledness and discord on the other is,
hypothetically, explained by a past occurrence which introduced a
movement opposed to harmonious structurization. This could be
made to sound nicely scientific—but as related to the inward aspect
of the human experience it becomes a legend.

Moreover, there exists about historical events a scale of *inner
relevancy.* This scale mounts in the direction from natural to secular to sacred history. Whether polymerization occurred in this or
in that way subsequent to the clustering of atoms, whether the birds
branched off the reptiles in this or that fashion or at this or that
period has no relevancy to my being. No matter how much I may
be interested in evolution—as far as the immediate questions of my

---

[3] I am using the terms "explaining" and "comprehending" in the sense in
which Karl Jaspers has used them in a different connection; the meaning is
obvious from the present context.

personal life go, I could not care less. Not so with secular history. The battle of Philippi, the Thirty Years' War, the American Revolution are more personally relevant. They have shaped, no matter how remotely, my life. The question as to their veracity has a certain indirect bearing on me, at least *causally*. The intended sacrifice on Mount Moriah, the consummated sacrifice of Mount Golgatha, the Resurrection—these are events of the *highest* personal significance, of *final* significance. Every life is *interiorly related* to these events with an immediacy which makes even secular history seem pale by comparison. Whether those events of sacred history are true at all, whether they occurred as told—nothing could be more personally relevant than these questions.

Will the two worlds of which we spoke initially, the world of objectivation and the world of inwardness, forever remain incompatible? Will, with the progress of science, the Cartesian chasm be further widened and man still more fearfully alienated from himself? The victory in our time, of dialectic materialism in the East and of positivism in the West, seems to indicate just that.

This is precisely where men like Father Teilhard come in. Teilhard's most original and persistent idea, that of complexity-consciousness, amounts to nothing less than a formal attempt at a welding, a confluence of the world as *res extensa* and the world as *res cogitans*. The very term "complexity-consciousness" symbolizes this quite neatly. Together with this goes, quite logically, his other central theme: the *hierarchic structure* and *polarized flux* of the universe. Thus, Father Teilhard's work—though tentative and fragmentary—will remain as a great sign to show that we are in the middle of a crisis, a wholesome crisis that ought to heal the split in our soul. No matter how many of the details of Teilhard's work may succumb to later criticism (this is not important) his chief impulse is anti-Manichaean. And this is of a significance which cannot be underestimated.

Even a man like Teilhard de Chardin will never completely succeed in welding faith and science by a formalized procedure. It is a good thing that should be so. But he has fully welded them in the depth of his own person. This created loneliness. He was a man misunderstood by his fellow scientists and his fellow theologians alike. From all that has been remarked here it is quite understand-

able why some scientists regard *The Phenomenon of Man* as un-
scientific and some theologians regard it as unsound. Pascal once
remarked that Christ is in a no-man's-land, rejected by Jews and
Gentiles alike. This no-man's-land is today, more than ever, the
natural habitat of the *Chrétien engagé*. There is about all Teilhard's attempt at reconciliation something deeply touching. Compared with it so many of the hackneyed treatises on science and
religion (by skeptics and scholastics alike) seem like cold intellectual
games. In Father Teilhard's work one feels a movement of love, like
that of a language interpreter who frantically tries to help two op-
posing camps to come at least to a linguistic entente. Even his terminology betrays this, and one cannot remain unmoved. (The term
"Omega point" has a scientific connotation—the symbol of Greek
letter and "point" suggests a graph—and at the same time an evident
scriptural connotation. It is the language of love which creates
these semantic bridges.) The interpreter from no-man's-land, rush-
ing frantically back and forth, is bound to appear as a traitor, once
to this camp and then to the other. This, too, is one of the marks of
the *Chrétien engagé*, and cannot be avoided. The heroic attempt
to bring hostile armies to meet on a terrain of truth makes the go-
between appear as a dual spy. His language is bound to slip. Hence
we should not be surprised if Father Teilhard talks at one time like
any one of a dozen of his scientific colleagues.

Left for a long time to itself, under the prolonged and universal
play of chance, matter manifests the property of arranging itself in
groupings which are more and more complex and, at the same
time, more and more enclosed in consciousness. Once begun, this
double movement, coupled with cosmic involution (corpusculiza-
tion) and psychic interiorization (or "centration"), is continued, ac-
celerating and pushing itself forward as far as possible.

On other occasions he talks like this: "While masking a higher
stage in the gratuitousness of the divine operator, are not creation,
the Incarnation, and the Redemption each so many acts indis-
solubly linked in the apparition of participated being?" The first
quotation does not sound much different from statements by
Haeckel which had such bad influence on the church attendance of
the *fin de siècle* bourgeoisie. It is hard to believe that the second
quotation comes from the same pen. These are the hazards of the

conciliator. He is easily caught in cross fire. Compared with him the scholastic philosopher of our time is like a man tagging little paper flags on to colored maps.

Teilhard's idea that man is as yet embryonic and unfulfilled is also typical of a precarious role with dual commitments. As far as it is eschatologically inspired, it is Christian. As far as it is biologically inspired, it smacks of the nineteenth-century optimism of progress. As we have pointed out, the idea of progress by evolution is pragmatic. It becomes questionable the moment we introduce aesthetic and moral values. If we do this, we perceive heights and ebbs in history but no "cone." The cave drawings of ten thousand years ago are more "advanced" than all the academic art of Darwin's contemporaries. The sculpture and architecture of the nineteenth century are far below Greek sculpture and architecture two and a half thousand years before. It is quite conceivable that our time, with its tremendous burst in technological progress, will in the judgment of history be related to the lowest phases of moral human development. Thus within recorded human history at least there is no unequivocal evolution. Moreover, the Christian fulfillment is entwined with history and, at the same time, mysteriously outside historical progression. While I am writing this, a state of sanctity is being attained by "little souls" anonymously scattered on the globe. Ever since the Incarnation fulfillment is free, *hic et nunc*—it cannot wait for occurrences on the timetable of an external process. "Out of these stones God can make children of Abraham." The Paulinian idea of freedom from the law pertains also to the laws of historical sequence. The idea of an ultrasynthesized mankind which, as a developmental stage, represents the Mystical Body appears like Comtean optimism in a baptized version. It seems to go against the Paulinian idea of freedom. Such an externalized concept of cohesiveness does remind us of present-day forms of collectivism—no matter how much Father Teilhard and his commentators object to such interpretation. The spirit will always be fed from the twin sources of loneliness and society. The Garden of Gethsemane and the Upper Room are two typical images of our inspiration.

These critical observations are not made just for the sake of criticism. On the contrary. It is quite possible that later generations may look on Father Teilhard as a Saint Augustine of natural history.

The naïveté and the time-conditioned limitations of some of Teilhard's work favor this comparison. Saint Augustine was the first to introduce the Christocentric theme into human history. Father Teilhard does so with natural history. Many of the details of *De Civitate Dei* appear today just as naïve and time-conditioned as many aspects of Father Teilhard's work. Yet the genius of Augustine succeeded in introducing a metaphysical *timor* into the reading of history, and the idea of history as a drama with hidden content has never completely disappeared since then. It is quite conceivable that Teilhard de Chardin's *universum Dei* will mark the same milestone in the philosophy of nature.

Of course, the spiritual drama immanent in history was stated long before Saint Augustine—namely, in Scripture. Saint Augustine has only elaborated on it in the language of the historian and philosopher of his time. And something quite similar is true in the case of Father Teilhard. He has made the spiritual drama of cosmogenesis eminently palatable to the modern taste. But in a different language it has been stated long before. And, as in some of the best stories, the thrill is maintained although the whodunit has been given away on the first page: "In the beginning God created Heaven and Earth."

9

Jung and Teilhard

By Bernard Towers

The writings of Teilhard and Jung have many features in common, those of the one devoted to the macrocosm and the place of man in it; of the other to the microcosm, that is the individual man himself. When the story comes to be written of the development of science in the twentieth century it may well be found that here were two men who played decisive roles in rescuing the scientist, and hence mankind, from the self-contained contradictions to which the logic of the science of the nineteenth century must inevitably have led. The technique of science as it is commonly understood, the method of reductive analysis, that is the explanation of things and events solely in terms of their component parts and antecedents, will always be essential to any understanding of nature. But nineteenth-century scientists, particularly biologists, understandably in reaction against the deist-inspired natural theology of the previous century, fell into the error of supposing, as Epicurus did in his intellectual battles with Aristotle, that explanation in terms of material and efficient causes is not merely necessary (as Aristotle and all of us would agree), but is wholly adequate. The formal cause and the final cause have long been dismissed in the polite circles of "traditionalists" (as they are fast becoming) as purely metaphysical and hence, in the traditional view, quite meaningless abstractions.

One cannot but admire the vigor and enthusiasm with which the apostles of the materialist enlightenment pursued and pursue explanation according to what might be called the "nothing-but hypothesis": everything is to be "explained" as nothing but a composite of simpler things, themselves reducing to nothing but yet more formless things, until all is reduced to atoms and the void, ultimately chaos. Both Teilhard and Jung have known such apostles intimately in their own spheres of scientific inquiry, and have each borne eloquent testimony, sometimes verbal, sometimes silent, to the admiration and respect in which they have held their colleagues. Without such men the world would be much the poorer in human experience and in knowledge of nature. Accurate, objective analysis of a thing or an event is an essential first-step toward understanding it, but cannot of itself provide that understanding. The pathos that we sometimes discern today in the confident, enthusiastic writings of scientists of the past derives not only from our practical experience of some of the horrors of a scientific age wherein there ought, according to the prophets, to be only benefits and blessings, but also from a realization that all this was somehow necessary, a stage in growing up. Adventurous spirits a hundred years ago were proclaiming in the name of science the coming dawn of intellectual liberation and, pathetically enough, were welding ever stronger the chains of our present enslavement to a characteristically "scientific" outlook which is bound to lead the man who holds fast to it to disillusion and despair. Few men have the courage consciously to hold fast; most have too much common sense or too much *joie de vivre* ever to make the attempt, or even to feel the *angst* of the situation. But whatever one perceives, however vaguely, and thinks to be true, no matter how quickly and with what apparent effectiveness it is banished from the conscious mind, is never wholly lost to the personality. Indeed it may grow there, in the darkness of the unconscious, to prodigious size, and finally demand attention in a way that leaves the sufferer no option. It is well known that the class of scientific research workers provides a large number of patients for the various schools of depth analysis.

Both Jung and Teilhard have always claimed to be working in

the scientific field of phenomena, to be empirical scientists devoted to purely objective observation, insofar as any observation is ever purely objective—except it be trivial; devoted to the construction of hypotheses on the basis of the observations, and to the testing of the hypotheses by further examination of phenomena in themselves. Each has insisted, however, that true impartiality demands that *all* phenomena be observed and noted, not simply those that are more readily accounted for in terms of current scientific dogma. Such an attitude is inevitable for a student of the whole, whether the whole is the cosmos itself or the psyche of individual human beings. But the conclusions have been so different from those arrived at in the more usual type of inquiry made by biological scientists, that both Teilhard and Jung have been bitterly accused, by some of their critics, of treason to the cause of science; sometimes contemptuously dismissed as unreliable, outside the scientific pale.

Perhaps the trouble is mainly due to the reintroduction by both of them of the concept of purpose into their accounts of the phenomena they have studied. How distasteful this must be to many heirs of nineteenth-century rationalism can be imagined from a statement made in 1876 by the great E. Du Bois-Reymond [1]: "The possibility, ever so distant, of banishing from nature its seeming purpose, and putting a blind necessity everywhere in the place of final causes, appears, therefore, as one of the greatest advances in the world of thought, from which a new era will be dated in the treatment of these problems. To have somewhat eased the torture of the intellect which ponders over the world problem will, as long as philosophical naturalists exist, be Charles Darwin's greatest title to glory." But the purpose discerned by our two modern authors is of a different kind from that against which the above protest was made.[2] The purposes seen in natural events by deists of the eighteenth century such as Paley were extrinsic in character, imposed on nature from without by a wholly transcendent deity. The purpose that Jung sees operating within the human psyche is, like that perceived by Teilhard to be operating at the core of the cosmos, intrinsic in character and essentially immanent, immanent in the sense

---

[1] *Darwin versus Galiani* (Berlin: 1876).
[2] For discussion of the meanings of telos see my article, "Teleology and the Anatomist," *Blackfriars*, 1957, No. 38, pp. 355-64 and pp. 408-17.

and to the extent that it can be legitimately studied by the methods of natural science.

The story of evolution is the story of the working out of this purpose. Jung is concerned more particularly with the ontogenetic evolution of the psyche, though his theory of the collective unconscious necessarily involves some consideration of phylogeny. For Teilhard a similar sense of immanent purpose imposes itself as a result of study of the evolution of the cosmos: his theme is that of the phylogenetic development of man. It is in and through man that this purpose becomes finally manifest. Once perceived in man, this same purpose is seen as necessarily operating throughout all the countless years of evolutionary time that have led to man. The whole cosmos becomes involved, just as, in ontogenetic development of the psyche, all parts of the individual's environment are necessarily involved in the formation of the personality. Man is inconceivable without the cooperation of the whole of nature: deprive him of any one of a dozen simple chemical elements, and inevitably his biological existence comes to an end. Deprive him of plant forms and again, together with the rest of the animal kingdom, he would cease to be. Deprive him of any major part of his normal environment, and his intellectual, moral, and aesthetic life would not be, would never have been, possible: where would be the apparatus of the special senses if there were or had been nothing for the special senses to respond to? Deprive him of the past, and he would never have begun to know the story of his evolution, of his place in nature: it seems that, when one contemplates nature in the round, so to speak, one sees that "they also serve who only stand and wait," even if they have to wait for hundreds of millions of years before being discovered by the paleontologist.

The goal of life in Jung's eyes is the birth and development, the realization, one might say, of what he has called the self. For Teilhard the goal is the birth and development, the realization again, in mankind as a whole, and hence in the cosmos as a whole, of what he has called Omega. The concept of Omega has suffered serious misinterpretation in the hands of hostile critics, both scientific and theological. Not a few have been inclined to dismiss Teilhard as no more than yet another of those emergent evolutionists whose views have provoked moderate interest from time to time ever since

the theory of evolution became a happy hunting ground for speculative thinkers. They have tried to account for the appeal which
his works are evidently having for so many people, who would not
have been taken in by his predecessors, on the basis of a current
widespread anxiety about future international relations and of the
anxious need for a new optimism to fill the void created by the disillusion of the last two decades. But Teilhard, it seems to me, is in
no way visualizing a slow emergence of some God-in-the-future, the
emergence of God out of something not-God or out of something
that could be called God only in a pantheistic framework which he
expressly repudiates. For Teilhard, God is an ever-living and ever-
present reality. He is the source of all being and, in particular, the
source of that evolutionary force which, from the beginning of time
so far as we can judge, has been gathering momentum against the
force of that other stream which we discern in the cosmos, that
which leads to increasing entropy. It is significant that Teilhard
chose precisely the word Omega in his attempt to convey his meaning. The word carries in one sense, it is true, the meaning of an
end-result, a result-in-time, such as has been postulated by emergent
evolutionists. But it also implies an end-in-view and, like all such
ends, must be in some sense present already. But not only as an
idea. Teilhard lays great stress on the fact of Omega as a living reality here and now, a force that has always been. The word Omega
is emptied of its most significant meaning if it does not carry with
it the sense of Alpha. Alpha and Omega are two aspects of the
creator, who is at once immanent in the evolving cosmos and at the
same time transcendent to it. The "emergence," then, of Omega,
which Teilhard sees as the major feature of human progress in the
future, is an emergence in the proper sense of the term—namely, a
birth or realization of something already in existence but hitherto
hidden from view (one makes no reference to the question of the
possibility, or the fact, of divine revelation) known in a sense only
to mother nature. At Omega point, mankind as a whole will have
come to know and accept nature, to know and accept itself, to know
and accept God; men united in the charity of understanding, united
in the love of all of nature through which they have come to be
and without which they would be nothing, united in love of one
another, united in love of the God who is Alpha and Omega, the

source of all being. The parallel with the birth of the Self in on-
togeny is illuminating: the labor in the one case belongs to the
individual alone, in the other it is, in Saint Paul's words, "the whole
of nature" which "groaneth in travail."

It is in the notion of a turning-in toward a center already necessarily existent within, that *enroulement* which Teilhard saw as the
essential feature of the evolutionary process, that we perceive strong
echoes of Jung, for whom the individuation process in the second
half of life, is again an *enroulement* in search of the center of the
personality. Though a center, the Self is at the same time, fittingly
enough, the whole. Jung himself has devoted most of his studies to
this task of the second half of life, to the final achieving of the goal
of individual psychic evolution. This is probably because the problems that arise in this phase of development have been precisely
what have induced the majority of Jung's patients to seek his aid.
Jung is first and foremost a clinician, and his system of thought is
the result of a doctor's attempt both to account for his patients'
symptoms and signs and to alleviate their sufferings, their dis-ease.
Now it is always dangerous to argue from a study of pathological
cases of limited variety to the nature of the normal, especially when
the subject of inquiry is one so difficult and complex as the nature
of man himself. But in the present early days of depth psychology
such shortcomings in theory as might result are, perhaps, inevitable,
because in the very nature of things the majority of practicing therapists will themselves be one-time patients (in the real sense of the
word "patient"), who have achieved whatever maturity and balance
they may possess only through a conscientious working-through, in
analysis, of their own emotional conflicts and difficulties. The practical experience of analyzing the various factors that contributed to
a former, frank neurosis, is sometimes regarded as somehow necessary to the making of an analyst. But the argument is clearly false.
There is no necessary correlation between the degree of understanding that might be attained and the intensity of personal suffering
formerly experienced.

Here we meet with the first of two marked differences between
the thought of Teilhard and that of Jung, with which it is intended
to close this brief study. For Teilhard the process of *enroulement*,
leading eventually to Omega, is one which occurs naturally, accord-

ing to the pattern of the evolutionary process itself—although he recognizes that reflective man is capable now of choosing whether to cooperate in the process or to oppose it. He is optimistic enough to suppose that mankind will be neither foolish enough nor wicked enough to defeat the process when it is at last within sight of its goal. For Jung, on the other hand, the birth of the Self necessarily requires, it seems, the assistance of an analyst as accredited *accoucheur,* for, in his view, "the process of individuation is far from an automatic psychic development." [3] If this is indeed the case, and if, as seems possible, Teilhard's Omega point will not be reached until there are many more integrated and fully conscious individuals about than there are today, then clearly professional analysts are going to have an indispensable part to play. But perhaps it will be neither so simple, in one sense, nor so difficult, in another, as that. Jung himself has paid relatively little attention to the process of psychic evolution as it occurs in the first phase of the individual's life, except in so far as it may have been a faulty development, long since past, in the lives of those older patients who have sought his aid. It is in this earlier period that the Ego is differentiated, developed, and finally established. It is perhaps not unlikely that for many of the patients of analytical psychologists the dialogue between the Ego and the Unconscious, which is essential to the realization of the Self, has proved impracticable or impossible precisely because the Ego was never given a real chance to grow in the way that it must. But for some of those millions who never have cause to concern themselves with this sort of problem it might be quite different. In a comparatively recent paper Jacobi[4] has argued, apparently for the first time, that there may be "a natural process of individuation, occurring without the individual's awareness." She distinguishes this from that "deliberately furthered and more or less consciously experienced process of individuation," which is what Jung means by the term. It may be that there are many ways of discovering the Self. If many of us find it possible to accept and to integrate the unconscious only as adults and under guidance, it may

[3] Jung, C. G., *The Integration of the Personality* (London: Routledge and Kegan Paul, 1940), p. 32.

[4] Jacobi, J., "The Process of Individuation," *Journal of Analytical Psychology,* 1958, III, 95-114.

be that the majority of people shift for themselves and, in the normal course of development from infancy to maturity, "without benefit of any special technique or spiritual direction, achieve the wholeness and wisdom that is granted as the reward of a fully lived-out life" (*loc. cit.*). This is more in keeping with Teilhard's outlook than the views, usually rather gloomy, of many depth psychologists of all schools, concerning what happens to the psyche if it is left to grow and develop freely, unattended by a vigilant psychotherapist.

One other, and really fundamental, difference between Teilhard and Jung calls for mention in this essay. The conflict here, characteristically enough, is the basic one between the individual and the community. Teilhard looks forward ultimately to the development of a sort of world state, to a practical, existential unity of mankind in which individual desires and strivings will be freely forsaken for the benefit of the community; in which even the consciousness of individuals will somehow be subsumed in a collective "superconsciousness." This is one aspect of Omega point. For Jung, on the other hand, the whole aim of psychic existence is precisely to extricate oneself from the power of the collective: not, it is true, from a collective *super*conscious, but at any rate from that collective *un*conscious in which our psychic life is rooted. The whole of Jungian terminology is orientated toward the uniqueness of the personality, toward the elevation, salvation almost, of the individual. Islands of consciousness, representing the psyches of individuals, are visualized as rising out of the sea of the unconscious. The Jungian aim is to help each little island to become ever more aware, ever more understanding of itself, of the other islands around it, of the sea out of which they have all arisen. In this process the island will grow in area, and will rise higher out of the water. It will achieve greater form and significance, greater distinction. Throughout this development, and more particularly in the later stages, the person concerned will certainly develop more control over his own emotions and reactions, and more understanding of those of others. He will become more tolerant, more benign. But islands can never be other than alone. One who follows this path of "individuation" may well find himself becoming more and more isolated, more and more lonely in a very deep sense. To give oneself in love to another, and to inspire love in return, requires qualities quite other than calm and tolerant benignity. Seeking and finding the Self is, perhaps, an essential part of the task of achieving personal freedom. But freedom for what? If only to add a little extra bulk to the island of Self, and to help others to do the same, then the process, for all that it seems to lead to sweet reasonableness, is, quite literally, selfish; when the process goes wrong it becomes obviously selfish, as occurs in those unhappy cases of "inflation" of the personality.

The individuation process would not, one imagines, have been enough for Teilhard. At some point the Self must abandon itself to the Other. No restriction of individual liberty is here involved. Rather is this the achievement of the greatest liberty known to man, the freedom to dedicate oneself, whether to a spouse, to religion, to a social or a political movement, to any real vocation. Such dedication, idealism, love, is rightly suspect to analytical therapists, because so often affective states of this kind can be shown, on analysis, to have produced or to be the product of intolerable internal conflicts within the patient's psyche. But the final state of mankind, that of the collective superconscious, will be arrived at not as a result of unconscious "identification" and "introjection," but by the free dedication of whole and integrated personalities. It is likely, perhaps, that before mankind arrives at Omega point the "natural process of individuation" described by Jacobi will become the norm for many generations of men and women. The Jungian and other schools of depth psychology, having demonstrated the hazards to which the developing psyche is exposed, and having taught us how to avoid disaster, will have fulfilled their purpose. They will remain in the grateful memory of our descendants.

10

The Noosphere and Extrasensory Perception

By Vincent Cronin

If the noosphere is to evolve in conformity with earlier cosmic developments, we may expect on the one hand keener perception of the external world and on the other improved communication between persons. Greater knowledge and awareness are dependent not only on clarity and logic of thought but on the improved quality and wider range of human perceptions.

At the present stage of evolution further cerebralization is limited by the crass and rudimentary nature of man's sense organs. Yet Father Teilhard suggests that man's physical as opposed to psychic development is all but complete. Man may become taller and longer-limbed, with a corresponding slight increase in the extent of his nervous system, but he is unlikely to evolve a third physical eye or ear to permit sight in greater depth or stereophonic hearing.

Along what lines then is man's evolution to continue? Partly, answers Father Teilhard, by interchange of knowledge and by team research. But a team no less than a single individual is limited by its mode of perception. It seems difficult to imagine the continued evolution of the noosphere without some radical development of means of communication. Unity, unanimity—the words occur often in *The Phenomenon of Man*—yet both are dependent on communication, a problem Father Teilhard seldom discusses. It is my belief that extrasensory perception may be one of the means toward which man is groping in his search for improved communication with other psyches (and I include here non-human psyches).

Research into extrasensory perception, led by Myers in England and Rhine of Duke University in America, has now assembled a large body of evidence attesting the existence of at least three unusual phenomena. First, telepathy: communication between psyche and psyche otherwise than through the known channels of the senses, as at a distance without external means. Second, identification of a nearby but unseen object (for example, some persons when asked to identify cards placed face-downward register an exceptionally high number of correct guesses). Third, prediction. This can take many forms, notably awareness in a dream of a disaster about to overtake a person usually known to the dreamer.

These three forms of perception have during the last few years become so well established as to prove a serious embarrassment to traditional scientific theory. They seem to challenge at least two basic assumptions: that we can know nothing which is not first in our senses, and that perception is confined to the immediate present, although of course it can lead to implications about both past and future. Attempts therefore have been made to discredit Dr. Rhine's methods of sampling and to write off prediction as hysterical guesswork.

However, when we turn to our own experience, we find a good deal of evidence for believing in extrasensory perception. Between any two persons deeply in love there pass perceptions and awarenesses which do not seem to follow the pathways of sense. Sometimes a family or group will experience a unanimity over and above any expressed wishes of its members. Again, some people are known for their hunches and good luck: what are these but an ability to glimpse the future dimly but directly?

Though ESP embarrasses many scientists, it seems to tally remarkably well with Father Teilhard's theory of a psyche running through all matter. If we admit that ESP may be true and consider its phenomena within the context of Father Teilhard's noosphere, we see that they satisfy this demand for "the closer association of the grains of thought" and increased interiorization. ESP, in fact, partially liberates the body from the limitations of matter. It does so in two ways: first, as mentioned above, by freeing the individual from the limitations of his senses which, after all, have been evolved chiefly to satisfy animal needs. Instead of peering as it were through the chinks of a tight armor, by means of ESP man is able, today only for short periods in rare circumstances but perhaps in future centuries for long periods of time or even totally, to discard his armor altogether, so as to perceive objects directly with his psyche. Secondly, as a member of something greater than himself, the noosphere, he is able to free himself from the limitations of words. I am thinking here not chiefly of the diversity of languages in the five continents, perhaps the greatest of all barriers to a world society, but of the limitations of language as such: the fact, for instance, that its very structure makes it a poor vehicle for the description of reality, particularly spiritual reality. (One cannot help being impressed by Father Teilhard's own difficulties and tentative neologisms, and, at another level, by the frequent failure of spiritual writers to communicate their meaning, even in poetry.) As the noosphere becomes more and more interiorized, we can expect subtler and subtler nuances of awareness, which language will be increasingly at a loss to express. Further evolution seems to demand some more exact and direct form of communication than the sounds made by tongue and lips, and heard by an ear far less subtle in its discrimination of tones than the ears of certain animals.

If ESP is not just a branch-line of evolution but a hesitant forward groping by the main stem, we may begin to picture a new future stage of the noosphere. Direct perception of objects by the psyche, direct intercommunication of one psyche with another and with a group, ability of the psyche to leap the barriers of the present—at least for a limited period of time—and perceive directly some future events.

Now this picture for all its strangeness is not totally strange. Already the schoolmen of the Middle Ages were sketching some such picture of life, not among men but among the angels. The angel, being incorporeal, perceives directly with his mind. He can assume human or quasi-human form, but is not limited thereby. He often communicates directly with man's psyche, for instance in dreams, and, knowing the future, he can act as a trustworthy guide to man.

Now between present-day man and point Omega there is only one stage for which we have any evidence: the choir of angels. Is it surprising then that man on his way to Omega should evolve along a line at one point of which he will come into possession of some at least of the qualities which theologians (not in any arbitrary manner but from a study of man himself, Scripture, and the scale of being) have assumed to characterize the angelic orders?

I have said that ESP permits us to get into more direct touch with other psyches, human and non-human. At another and more important level, the level of infused grace, it also permits us to get into direct touch with God. For it is nothing less than the way taken by many contemplatives, visionaries, and mystics. Now the fact that mystical experience is granted comparatively rarely and to comparatively few persons may well be *partially* dependent on this: that we have not yet as a race evolved to the level of habitual extrasensory perception. Should the day dawn when man does arrive at such a level and becomes in certain respects angelic, then is it too fanciful to hope that he may, even in his life on earth, be granted glimpses of the Godhead that are better than analogical? Then indeed man could claim with justice to be only a little lower than the angels.

Such at least is one possible way of envisaging man's continued evolution, under grace, toward God.

11

"Thy Labour Under the Sun"

By C. C. Martindale

Ecclesiastes (9:10) says: "Whatsoever thy hand findeth to do, do it with thy might" (Vulgate: "earnestly"), but for just the opposite reason to that which a Christian would offer—Ecclesiastes considers that when the body dies there will be no awareness "in the grave towards which thou art hastening." But it is quite possible to draw a hardly less false conclusion from the certainty that we shall be very much "aware" when the body has died. I was once trying to get a clever but exasperatingly pious boy to take trouble over his Latin verses. "What'll be the use of Latin verses," he replied, "at the Day of Judgment?" Rather later, in a "religious" establishment, I was trying to find, as a starting-point, what a young student was specially interested in. He said: "But ought we to have special interests?" Well, if he had none, could he sympathize with others who *had* interests? Would not his apostolic life be singularly narrowed?

These thoughts have been touched off by reading some pages by Father Teilhard about "The Divinization of Our Activities" in *Le Milieu Divin*—pages which should suffice to rescue any reader from that kind of defeatist pietism to which I have been alluding.

How, then, deal with this world? Saint Paul says we must do all —"eat or drink"—in the name of Christ. But I can't think of that explicitly all the time! Will a "supernatural intention," formed for instance when I wake up, be adequate? A general "right intention" is no doubt needed; but shall we be satisfied with it? I want to be more lastingly conscious of serving and pleasing God than just making a "morning offering" and then devoting myself to work or play. Yet does that not risk my concentrating on God turning into contempt for that very work—let alone play? "Vanity of vanities": all so much dust to be blown away when I die, leaving just God and myself? But what *is* that "self"? Father Teilhard never tires of reminding us that we live in a universe and are part of it. An enormous history has fashioned my heredity, my environment, my education: "What *entered into thee*—That was, is and shall be"— even at school, I was deeply shaken by that line of Browning's: even when I shall be in the abnormal state of "disembodied spirit," my soul will not be just "soul" in general, any more than my body, when its "resurrection" has taken place, will be just "body" in general, but *I*, body-soul, will be my complex self—purified, please God, and glorified—but my "works will have followed me."

But more: the world is not yet complete. I, enmeshed in this web of cosmic influences, am not only formed, but formative: I hinder or help the future. I prevent, or make progress toward the "kingdoms of this world" becoming the "kingdom of the Lord and of His Christ" (Apocalypse, 11:15). In what follows, we have to express ourselves in such words as are available to us, and even the sublimest poet knows that what he says comes nowhere near his vision; the artist is almost ready to cry, so far is what he has painted from what he has "seen"; Saint Thomas, toward the end of his life, had some consciousness of the "really Real" that he felt ready to disavow what he had written and did indeed scratch out a lot of it. Saint John, in the Apocalypse (8:1—which should really be 7:18), having symbolized the course of the world as the breaking of seven Seals, when he reaches the Consummation, the breaking of the Seventh Seal, gives up human language altogether and can say only that there was "silence in heaven." So no one will be likely to call Father Teilhard a materialist! But, when speaking of such matters, it is hard not to sound pantheist, at least at times. (Yet Saint John of the Cross, supreme mystic and ascetic, and nicknamed Apostle of Nothingness so often did he insist that created things were nothing and must be discarded, was nonetheless a marvelous poet, drew with startling realism, loved the rocky landscape of Castile, and liked asparagus. . . .)

Well, it is granted by all Christians that man, who is spiritual, exists for God. But into us, who in eternity are to be body-soul, all material creation has entered and we are entering into it. Hence, since the Consummation is not yet reached, Saint Paul can say (Romans 8:22) that *all* creation is *still* "groaning and suffering birth-pangs *along with us* and joins in our yearning" for the ransom of our humanity. We agree that a certain timidity has been felt about this apparent equipping *all* creation with a sort of consciousness: even the late Monsignor Ronald Knox said that if Saint Paul was referring to the whole of creation, he must be speaking with "something of a poetic outlook."

But further, all this consummation is to be brought about through Christ. Read that amazing proclamation of what Christ is, and is to be, in Colossians (1:13-22): "Christ exists before all creation—yes! *in* him were created all things—things in heaven or on earth, things visible and invisible . . . by means of him, and unto him, they all of them are created . . . and in himself they all of them hold together." But since manifestly this has not yet been fulfilled, this is why Saint Paul can continue: "That is why I rejoice in my sufferings on your account, and make up from my side what is *lacking* in the pains of Christ, in *my* flesh, on behalf of *His* body—that is, the Church" (*ibid.*, 24). He longs to present every man mysteriously perfected in Christ: "Yes, for *this* I strain and struggle in the measure of that energy of *His* that energizes so mightily in *me*" (*ibid.*, 29). And it is Christ whom God has set to be "Head Supreme for the Church—that is, His body—the full-filling of Him who is *fulfilling Himself, fully, in all things*" (Ephesians, 1:23).

We have to be bold, not timid, well aware that neither in word nor thought can we express the "how" Christ is to be "All in all" (Colossians, 3:11). But the "that" is left by Saint Paul and Saint John, indisputable. Christ does not consider himself complete—fulfilled—without his Christians incorporate with him, and they draw up, with and in themselves, the whole of creation. There is to be one Mountain of God through which cascades the Holy Spirit; one Bride of Christ; one Temple, one Vine, one Bread. (I cannot consider, here, hell or the fallen angels—Christ is to be Head of that immeasurable spiritual world "above us" as well as of this "earth," now so dislocated and disintegrated, but destined somehow to be unified in him. Much escapes our intelligence, but what God has revealed is "for us men and *our* salvation.") I may have strayed from the extract quoted at the beginning, but not, I hope, from the line of thought of my old friend—so happy (even so gay and *invigorating* a man) who died suddenly on—as he said he hoped to—the Day of Resurrection, Easter Sunday, 1955. "Bruised, but not broken . . . stoned, but never slain . . . for we look not on things visible, but on things unseen."

12

Teilhard in Fiction

By Geoffrey Wagner

The long philosophical novel with which Romain Gary won the Prix Goncourt essentially extends and elaborates the shorter book by virtue of which he gained the Prix des Critiques over a decade before. But it is a far grander opus than *A European Education,* even than the revised version, it is "a book that will keep us company for a long, long time" as André Malraux has put it. It is the contention of this note that it is so very largely thanks to the ideas of Pierre Teilhard de Chardin.

The structure of *The Roots of Heaven* is reminiscent of the style of another expatriate Pole—namely, Joseph Conrad: that is to say, the theme predominates over the characters as with Conrad. This is testified by the fact that in *The Roots of Heaven* the reader is told of the conclusion of characters often before he meets them. This has the kind of verisimilitude Conrad enjoyed playing with most elaborately (and that Gide learned at Conrad's hands, among others): for example, in Gary's epic we learn of Minna's abandoned jeep before being taken back to the start of her story. This, Conrad felt, is entirely like life, fragmentary and chaotic. We experience the reality along with the characters.

As a host of critics have shown, Conrad's difficulty was to save his characters from becoming postulates (or from being "flat," in E. M.

Forster's phraseology). Gary succeeds in *The Roots of Heaven,* as he does not in *Lady L,* because of his firsthand knowledge of equatorial African officialdom (I am thinking of obviously authentic characterizations like Schölscher, the Camel Corps official who turns Trappist in the book—symbolically, as Schölscher himself reflects, he is more exposed to the stars than normal men, and so closer to God). I would further point out in this connection that Minna, the least firsthand of all the characters, is surely the least real of them all;[1] she is introduced in the first place, I think, because Morel—the central Christ-figure—must have a German close to him, i.e., a fellow sufferer of the race that so made him suffer in the war.

The Conradian structure, especially in the Marlow books, is really one long confessional which gives the effect of quasi-biblical distance to the protagonist (e.g. *Lord Jim*); Gary's *The Roots of Heaven* is also a long confession, via reports, reports on reports, and so on, to Father Tassin, an unorthodox Jesuit priest with explicit physical and theoretical similarities to Pierre Teilhard de Chardin, a man who admired Gary's first novel and who, as we know, spent part of his paleontological career in the part of Africa in which the book is set. The two names, moreover, begin with the same letter.

Tassin's interlocutor is for the major part of Gary's text the reader's go-between, Saint-Denis, a local administrator who "rises" on the mention of Morel with "devotion" (p. 79) and has been "raised from the dead" (p. 89) by a native witch doctor.[2] Saint-Denis is the John the Baptist of the story, the man who gives testimony of Morel to Tassin and who eventually, so he says, wishes to be turned into a tree, a classical metamorphosis that Dante developed from Vergil, Spenser from Dante, and all from primitive culture rituals of the type Gary is hinting at here.

[1] Nor, frankly, is Minna at all carefully worked out. I computed that she was sixteen or seventeen when raped by the Russians (1945): she is twenty-three at the start of the novel (1951): but Eisenhower, who is referred to as Ike and as inhabiting the White House, did not become President until 1952.

[2] My page numbers refer to the following edition: Romain Gary, *The Roots of Heaven,* translated from the French by Jonathan Griffin (New York: Simon & Schuster, 1958). It is necessary to insert this provenance since, unlike most authors, the polyglot Gary takes a lively interest in, and frequently interferes with, his foreign translations. Nor do the pages in the English and American editions always tally.

Before proceeding to Gary's depiction of Father Teilhard in Tassin, however, it is necessary to enter several caveats qua method: thus, it would be quite impossible for anyone to have overheard or reported the lonely conversation between Youssef and Morel, wherein allegiance to the human race is shown as overcoming that to one particular race (p. 353). Again, the linguistic abilities of the characters (represented in the film by the majority speaking in thick foreign accents[3]) are unlikely to the point of unreality: they are those of the author, rather than of his characters; it is extremely unlikely that the American Forsythe and the British Colonel Babcock, a relic of the old order (p. 46, and p. 71), would both be at home in French and German.

Nevertheless, although Gary takes exceptional liberties with his method, the characterization of Teilhard-Tassin subsumes the whole work and charmingly contrasts with the orthodox, intellectually limited, yet also sympathetic, Father Fargue (p. 145 and p. 186).

It is with a tremendous debt to Teilhard that *The Roots of Heaven* opens and it closes with his compassionate shadow thrown over heterodox religion: I refer to the explicit union in "belief," at the end, of both the Moslem tracker Idriss, the man of instinct, and the Jewish photographer Fields, whose purely scientific preoccupations (getting a "good shot," etc.) provide a cold backdrop against which the author can make the elephant massacre all the more moving.

Tassin-Teilhard gives protection to Morel at the close (p. 361), but he himself rides on alone "in the absence of doubt and in the certainty of a final discovery." Professor Andrée Kail attaches more emphasis to this final granting of shelter than I can, for it is only a hinted probability, and Tassin remains independent of Morel.[4]

However this may be, Tassin is in general terms a fairly standardized conception of Father Teilhard. He provides the frame for the book and does not much participate in its actions in front of us. Yet his whole attitude is thoroughly Teilhardian when, right at the start, we learn that Tassin's writings "represented salvation as a

[3] See Patrick Leigh Fermor's "Making a Film in Africa," *The Sunday Times*, September 14, 1958, p. 12.

[4] Kail, Andrée M. F. "Le Symbole dans *Les Racines du Ciel*," *French Review*, October, 1958.

mere "biological mutation" (p. 43) and, as regards the practice of priesthood, that "he had long ago given up the small routines of his calling." When Saint-Denis thinks that the learned Father is telling his beads, we are told that Tassin uses his rosary merely to keep his fingers busy on the veldt and to help him smoke less (p. 226).

It would be supererogatory to make any point-for-point comparison between Teilhard's philosophy and that of Tassin in *The Roots of Heaven* for a number of reasons: first, Gary has only, in all justice, sketched in the characterization; second, he has completely taken over Teilhard's view for his personification, who in fact creates his title since he is a priest (heaven) passionately interested in excavation (roots); third, the whole of Gary's theme can be found in Teilhardian works like *L'Apparition de l'Homme, La Vision du Passé, L'Avenir de l'Homme*, and, finally, *Le Phénomène Humain.* This third reason is not intended as a denigration of Gary's achievement, so much as a tribute to Teilhard's enormously powerful influence. Frankly, Gary's whole idea of elephants as heroic individuals (especially pp. 60-1, 92, 106, 114, and 337-8) can be found summarized in the sections on The Transit to Life or The Expansion of Life in *The Phenomenon.* For Teilhard advanced the idea—extremely important to Gary's thesis—that the huge Pliocene animals, or *mammifères placentaires*,[5] represented the first stage in *hominization;* they were the first great individualists, like Gary's elephants, the first to start the phase of *speciation* and they were accordingly vast, in order to rise out of the primeval slime around them, and to triumph over the serpent. This somewhat vulgar oversimplification of what Father Teilhard in *The Phenomenon* (p. 89) called the "essential changeover between two states or forms of consciousness" is, all the same, what makes him refer with a kind of glowing pride to elephants in a number of places in his *œuvre.* What Gary does is essentially to put a kind of Rousseauvian hold on this theory of life. With him nature and liberty are synonymous, as Peer Qvist once remarks (p. 205), and he is clever in suggesting that the anachronistic nature of the elephant today is really similar to man's total liberty, if such were allowed in the "civilized" world. In other words, we are ignorant of the real extent of our freedom which is itself a kind of elephant today. As a matter of fact, Gary

[5] See *La Vision du Passé,* where Teilhard defines what he means by this term.

accords the name of De Vries, a paleontologist discussed by Teilhard in the *Revue des étudiants de l'Université Nationale de Péking* for 1932, to one of his most unpleasant characters, a butcher of elephants who hates life and is described as "the enemy of nature" (p. 8 and p. 10). For Gary as for Teilhard the elephants are an *image of liberty* (p. 31) and Gary's passages referring to them bringing a smile to one's lips (p. 92) could be matched by a passage on Pliocene animals in *The Phenomenon* (p. 157):

> Surely such luxuriance, such achievement, must precisely serve to condemn the future of these magnificent creatures, marking them for an early death, writing them off—despite their psychic vitality —as forms that have got into a morphological dead end.[6]

I have suggested that Teilhard's shadow lies over this noble work by Romain Gary, and I should like to conclude on this note. Morel may be a kind of Christ, with his disciples in men such as Forsythe, Fields, the silent Baron, the bus-driver, and various others who fade out in the fiction and who prominently include a Schweitzer in Peer Qvist (pp. 113-15); we have a Magdalen in Minna (p. 341), a Judas in Waïtari, and it is even true that Idriss suffers a kind of Pauline conversion (p. 198). But despite these many biblical parallels the author's attitude toward Morel still strikes me as highly ambivalent; Morel's quixotry is not wholly approved, and is indeed satirized on a lower level in the depiction of Armand Denis in *Lady L.*

It is Tassin who closes the work, we must remember, "in the absence of doubt and the certainty of a final discovery." What exactly is this final discovery? For we are explicitly informed, with all the emphasis of the book's concluding passages, that Tassin had "lived one of the finest and most interesting spiritual adventures a creature can have on earth" (p. 372).

Essentially, this is to know what it is to be human. Tassin has witnessed in Morel a true Teilhardian individual, a living anachronism, just as earlier in the book the police officer had required a boy of the Oulé tribe to stand in front of him for a moment, to remind him what humanity was, after the viciousness of the "civilized" Orsini.

---

[6] See also Alan Moorehead's *No Room in the Ark* (New York: Harper & Row, 1960), where we learn that about 90 per cent of the wild animals in Africa a century ago have today been destroyed.

But more than this Tassin's discovery is Teilhard's creation ideal, the identification of, and witness to, complete freedom in the natural world, to God's words in his works. As this is summarized in one passage (p. 52):

Schölscher was on the point of replying that men needed another company than their own kind, that they craved it desperately, like an almost physical presence, and that nothing on earth seemed big enough to satisfy that urge, those roots of heaven, as Islam called them, which were for ever gripping and torturing man's heart. . . .

13

The First Teilhard Symposium

By Dorothy Poulain

Halfway between St. Lô and Coutances on a grassy slope facing distant pasture lands is the Château de Cerisy with its old moat and huge Norman walls.

Here, Madame Heurgon, daughter of the late Paul Desjardins, has succeeded in reviving the celebrated "Décades" of the Abbaye de Pontigny inaugurated by her father between the two world wars. It was her idea that in 1958 one be dedicated to *La Pensée de Pierre Teilhard de Chardin*.

This was the first time since 1955 when the great Jesuit paleontologist had his "changement d'état" (as he referred to death) that a group of scientists, philosophers, and theologians gathered in a symposium to discuss the many aspects of his rich and complex thought. The significance of the occasion was not lost on those informed of the event (which, designedly, received no publicity), and it brought eager response from the Ivory Coast, from Algeria, Belgium, Germany, Luxembourg, Italy, and Spain. In all, the participants numbered about forty.

The Décade was presided over by Madame Jacques Madaule who is now writing a thesis on Teilhard. Her charm, competence, and devotion became apparent at once, and never failed her during our stay.

It had been decided, judiciously, to present the man, the thinker, before his thought; and for this purpose several of Teilhard's intimates had come to give their personal testimony.

The first of these was Mademoiselle Marguerite Teillhard-Chambon, his cousin, who, under her pen name of Claude Aragonnès, edited his *Lettres de Voyage*. At once we were transported into the world of Teilhard's childhood. We saw the ancestral home, a *gentilhommière* at Sarcenat in the austere Auvergne where Pierre, fourth of eleven children, was born on May 1, 1881. Then we learned to our surprise that his devout mother, to whom he was deeply attached, was the great-granddaughter of a niece of Voltaire. And our surprise increased on hearing that as a very small boy Teilhard developed a passion for the *hardest* objects he could find. These were usually pieces of iron picked up in the countryside, one of his most treasured possessions being an old horseshoe. This odd taste was the child's attempt, apparently, to associate the Absolute with something tangible, durable, imperishable.

After a happy home life we heard how he entered the Jesuit novitiate at eighteen, and later as a stretcher bearer in the trenches of the First World War humbly refused honors or promotions that were his due. We followed each phase of his extraordinary career till it ended as he—predestined priest of the Resurrection—always hoped it would, on a joyous Easter Sunday.

The program proper began with the scientists. Among them were Dr. Paul Chauchard, the neurophysiologist, Assistant Director of the École des Hautes Études, author of *La Foi du Savant Chrétien, La Création Evolutive*, and many other works; the Jesuit, Père François Russo, who commented on a number of Teilhard's unpublished texts, and stressed the point that research is evolution's present spearhead; the paleontologists, Dr. Crusafont Pairó, Teilhard's ardent champion in Spain, and Professor Piveteau of the Sorbonne, for whom Teilhard is one of the greatest minds that ever was, who read a paper on anthropogenesis.

There was presented then, in a magnificent panorama, a vision of the past on this lonely earth before man came, the millions of years when matter was being vitalized and its more complex forms which were destined to cradle the coming humanity emerged gropingly, awkwardly, and perfected their ultimate pattern.

There were usually two sessions a day, followed by discussion periods which became increasingly animated as the philosophers entered the arena. Père d'Armagnac, S.J., effected the transition with a paper, "The Philosophy of Nature," in which he made clear that in the creative action of God there is both mechanism and finality—the one horizontal, acting on the early stages of the universe, the other vertical revealing man in whom self-consciousness is the absolutely new element.

It became increasingly evident as the speakers succeeded each other that Teilhard's thought is both rational and superrational. His intention was to respond dialectically to the anguish of the modern world and to a humanism closed in on itself (Marxism, Existentialism). Though himself a Doctor of Theology, he abandoned the Scholastic vocabulary in order to make himself more accessible in scientific terms to the man of today, and this has greatly disturbed his critics of the more classic tradition. Nevertheless, the unsuspected number of persons brought into or back into the Church because of Teilhard's sympathetic understanding of their difficulties and his success in dissipating these would seem to speak for his more novel approach.

The problem of the *future* of man holds a very important place in Teilhard ("le Passé m'a révéle l'Avenir") and it is precisely this part of his work which has received the most criticism. Among the motives which explain the emphasis on the future is the recognition of a biological humanity; man is born not only as an *individual,* but as a *species.* It is in the noosphere, the "thinking envelope," that the individual solutions are contained.

With Père Wildiers, the Franciscan from Antwerp, the discussion entered the realm of the theologians; with Père de Lubac we left it, as he brought the Décade to a close with a superb paper on *Le Milieu Divin.* It is in this work that suffering, the problem of evil, and the purifying "passivities" are dealt with rather than in *Le Phénomène Humain,* which was written in a scientific discipline and *never intended as an explanation of the world.* But this is not the only cause of the too common misinterpretation of Père Teilhard's thinking. Basically, the chief cause of this confusion is the fatal hostility of those who, unable to perceive what is the essential question at a given moment of the world's history, see no reason why the question should be posed.

During the presentation of Christogenesis we were made aware of the fact that up to now and in spite of the dominant place Saint Paul gives to it, the third aspect or "nature" of Christ (difficult to classify as human or divine, but "cosmic"—as a result of the implications of the Incarnation) has hardly attracted the attention of the faithful or the theologians. But with the universe expanding fantastically before our eyes the time has come for Christianity to arouse itself to a distinct consciousness of what the dogma of the universality of Christ, transposed to these new dimensions, creates in the way of hopes and, at the same time, of difficulties.

Hopes because, if the Universe is so formidably vast and powerful, then thinking of Christ demands a frame of reference far more vast than that to which we have been accustomed. Difficulties because, if the new space-time concept demands this expansion of Christ, how can this come about without the loss of the adorable personality or the risk of seeing it volatilized? And here Teilhard finds the astonishing and liberating harmony between a religion of the Christic type and an evolution that is convergent. Were the world a static cosmos, relations of a conceptual or juridical order could be invoked to establish the primacy of Christ over Creation— Christ the King—because he has been so declared and not because any *organic* relation of dependence could conceivably exist between him and the fundamental irreducible multiplicity.

The central place this idea holds for Teilhard is found in a letter of capital importance written by him from Capetown, October 12, 1951, to the Superior General of the Society of Jesus in Rome. It was read to us at Cerisy by Père Le Roy, S.J., the biologist, as part of his personal testimony. With permission, I am using it here to conclude this account of the Décade:

VERY REVEREND FATHER,

On the point of leaving Africa (after two months of work and calm in the field), it seems that this is a propitious moment to let you know in a few words what is in my mind and how things are going with me.

(1) First of all I think you will have to be resigned to taking me

as I am—that is to say, with the congenital quality (or weakness)
which accounts for the fact that since childhood my spiritual life
has never ceased being completely dominated by a sort of profound
sentiment of the organic reality of the World; a sentiment at first
rather vague in my mind and heart, but gradually becoming with
the years a precise and invading sense of a general convergence
coinciding and culminating at its peak with the One *in quo omnia
constant* that the Society has taught me to love.

In the awareness of this movement and this synthesis of everything
in Xristo Jesu I have found an extraordinary and inexhaustible
source of inner light and strength, and an atmosphere outside of
which it has become impossible for me to breathe, adore, *believe.*
That which in my attitude for the past thirty years could be taken
for stubbornness or impertinence is merely the result of my being
unable to prevent my wonderment from manifesting itself.

This, psychologically, is the basic situation from which everything
derives, and that I can no more change than the number of my
years or the color of my eyes.

(2) With that made clear, and to reassure you of my inner position, I must insist on the fact that whether or not it is the case with
others the inner attitude I have just described has the direct effect
of binding me with increasing inevitability to three convictions
which form the very marrow of Christianity:

The unique value of man as the spearhead of Life; the axial position of Catholicism in the converging cluster of human activities;
and lastly, the essential perfecting function assumed by the risen
Christ in the center and at the summit of Creation. These three
elements have grown and continue to grow roots so deep and so
interwoven in the entire system of my intellectual and religious
vision that it would be impossible henceforth for me to uproot them
without destroying everything.

Truly, and by virtue of the whole structure of my thought, I feel
myself today more irretrievably bound to the hierarchical Church
and to the Christ of the Gospels than I have ever been at any moment of my life. Never has Christ seemed more real to me, more
personal, more immense.

How can anyone believe that the direction I have taken is a
wrong one?

(3) There remains the fact, and I acknowledge it fully, that Rome
can have its reasons for considering that, in its actual form, my
vision of Christianity is premature or incomplete and that as a
consequence it cannot be diffused at present without objections.

It is on this important point of outer fidelity and docility that
I want particularly (in fact that is the essential purpose of this letter) to assure you that in spite of certain appearances I am determined to remain "an obedient child."

Obviously, I cannot without risk of an inner catastrophe and of being unfaithful to my most cherished vocation, cease from my own seeking. But for several months I have no longer been concerned with the propagation but rather the *approfondissement* of my ideas. An attitude greatly facilitated for me by the fact that I can once again do direct scientific work.

These lines to my way of thinking are, I repeat, a simple laying bare of my conscience, and they await no answer from you. Try to see in them nothing but the proof that you can count on me entirely to work for the Kingdom of God which is the only thing I see and that interests me over and beyond the realm of Science.

Very respectfully your son in Christ,

P. TEILHARD DE CHARDIN

On returning home I reread *Le Christique,* Teilhard's spiritual testament written a month before his death. In a poignant passage, he writes:

How does it happen that, looking around me and still under the spell of what has become visible to me, I find myself practically alone of my kind? The only one to have *seen* . . . incapable, there-fore, when questioned, of citing a single author, a single piece of writing where, clearly expressed, one can recognize the marvelous "Diaphaneity" which for me has transfigured everything.

The eternal drama of the spiritual pioneer. One day may there be found place in our litanies for a special "Prayer for Precursors."

Part III

Teilhard's Vision

14

The Vision of Teilhard de Chardin:

A Radio Script by Neville Braybrooke

NARRATOR: Teilhard de Chardin spent his life digging up the past so that men might know more about the future. For he was at once both a strict Jesuit, and an explorer of prehistory; a naturalist of the open air, and a man of God who by his own personal detachment strove to enrich the lives of others. He knew all the religious paradoxes: the way forward that is the way back, or the way of renunciation which is really the way of development. These contraries in the spiritual life harmonized—like the in and out of breathing. But not in the spiritual life alone. He was fond of saying:

TEILHARD: There are times for growth and times for diminishment in the lives of each of us, just as there are, my friends, an infinity of vocations. In the Church too there's room for everyone—an Aquinas as well as a Mary Magdalen.

NARRATOR: The Church is often compared to a bark, Saint Peter's bark. Père Teilhard preferred to see the whole world as a ship, a kind of floating universe. Outward bound for the East, he reveled in the diversity of his fellow passengers and marveled at the human bond that unites all men—and their work.

Unbelievers, agnostics, skeptics—they were always among his friends. By an odd irony, they far outnumber the believers. If you read his letters, you will find that no term of endearment crops up so often as the word "friend."

Everywhere he went, he left friends behind him—often scientists who in the normal course of things saw his Church as the enemy of their calling. But here was a priest who was as loyal to science as he was to Christianity. Sir Julian Huxley probably speaks for many scientists when he sums up Teilhard as a dedicated Christian priest who felt it imperative to try to reconcile Christian theology with his views on evolution, and to relate the facts of religious experience to those of natural science. But if Teilhard spoke *to* scientists and humanists in a language that they could understand, he also spoke *for* waverers.

TEILHARD: By waverers I mean those inside and outside the Church who, instead of giving themselves wholly to the Church, hesitate on her threshold or turn away in the hope of going beyond her.

NARRATOR: In fact by a paradox that Teilhard would have loved, it is largely through the faith of unbelievers that his works have seen daylight. For during his life he submitted draft after draft of his books to his religious superiors, and time and again they were rejected. Yet he was not a follower of Saint Ignatius for nothing. He persisted, and those rejections—perhaps by another odd irony —enabled him constantly to revise and improve his manuscripts. Shooting manuscripts off to his superiors was rather like shooting arrows into the blue—and yet . . .

TEILHARD: If I didn't write, I should be a traitor. My prayer has always been "That we may be one," and my motto "We must dare all."

NARRATOR: So writing became for him with each rejection more and more an act of faith. As he told a cousin:

TEILHARD: I am a pilgrim of the future on the way back from a journey made entirely in the past.

[*Pause*]

NARRATOR: Here then is the course of his thought and life.

On May the 1st, 1881, Marie-Joseph-Pierre Teilhard de Chardin was born. His family were French country gentry, and from the windows of their chateau at Sarcenat you can see the capital of Auvergne, the vast green plain of Clermont, and the foothills of the Puy mountains.

TEILHARD: "You can see." How much depends on that phrase. Go back to your own beginnings and try to imagine how it was when you first opened your eyes and everything appeared jumbled up on one plane. A parable is there for the rest of life. I have repeatedly come back to it.

NARRATOR: His father was a naturalist who taught his eleven children to study wild flowers, insect life and rocks. Pierre was fast to learn.

TEILHARD: I suppose I was about six or seven when I used to potter off and collect bits and pieces. I hid a plow-key in a corner of our yard, I remember. I also hid some shell splinters. In retrospect, I now see that what drew me to hoard such relics was their durability. It came as a horrible shock to me when I realized that iron can be scratched and can rust.

NARRATOR: At ten he was sent to a Jesuit boarding school at Villefranche. His reports show he was frequently top of the class in various subjects, but nearly always bottom in religious instruction.

TEILHARD: I didn't care for the way that they put religion across. All that nonsense about God blessing Jesus and those goody-goody romances about the saints and martyrs. *Quelle fantasie!* What normal child would ever want to spend an everlasting life in such a company?

NARRATOR: (You can catch there the note of Voltaire from whom he was descended on his mother's side.)

TEILHARD: Yet when all is said and done this is only the repository side of religion. It has nothing to do with the Saint Vincent de Paul side—or with Pascal. All I know for sure is that by the time I was seventeen I was quite determined to join the Jesuit Order.

NARRATOR: A year later he entered the novitiate at Aix-en-Provence. His studies took him first to Laval in the west—and then north to Jersey. It was there, in the Channel Isles, that he underwent an inner crisis.

TEILHARD: I loved nature (by nature I mean scientific research) and I loved God. My problem was—can you love and serve both? I even seriously contemplated giving up my researches and told the Master of Novices so. He had a wonderful insight into my dilemma and explained to me how henceforth my service of God must push its way through scientific research to its extreme limit. So when they sent me off to Cairo to teach physics and chemistry at one of their colleges there, I went with a mind at peace. That was in 1905 when I was twenty-five.

NARRATOR: Three years later he was sent to England for the last stages of his training as a priest.

TEILHARD: How beautiful the autumns were at Hastings: the golden October days and the golden beaches. I can still hear the sea wind blowing over the downs and the cry of gulls over the cliffs. And it was at Hastings where I was reading theology that I became aware of the universe no longer as an abstract notion, but as a—how shall I put it?—but as a *presence*. It was something I would have to work out, but for the time being most of my concentration went on my divinity studies. Then on August the 24th, 1911, the feast day of Saint Bartholomew, the Apostle and patron of bookbinders, cheese merchants, dyers, leather workers, shoemakers and vine growers among other things, I was, at our French Jesuit House in Hastings, by his Lordship Bishop Amigo, and by the grace of God, ordained a priest.

NARRATOR: Shortly afterward it was back to Paris for formal training in paleontology, which is the study, among other things, of extinct organisms. Then in no time it was August, 1914—and war. Teilhard was quick to respond. He was enlisted as a stretcher bearer and there are many stories to be added to the medals he won for bravery. The North African sharpshooters of his regiment believed that he was protected by his *baraka,* a Moslem-Arabic word meaning "spiritual structure." (The word, incidentally, was often applied to Gandhi.) Max Bégouën, a fellow soldier of Teilhard's at the front, recalls his fearlessness.

MAX BÉGOUËN: I once asked him, how do you keep so calm in battle? Aren't you afraid of being shot? He smiled at me and said:

TEILHARD: If I'm killed I shall just change my state, that's all.

NARRATOR: Or there is the testimony of Max Bégouën's brother:

JACQUES BÉGOUËN: I was wounded and saw in the cross fire a stretcher bearer rise up before me. He bandaged me and carried me to the first-aid post. I thought that I had seen the appearance of a messenger from God.

NARRATOR: Later in the war (as we now know) Teilhard himself was to have a vision of Christ. When he writes about it he pretends that the vision is another soldier's story, but all the internal evidence goes to show that the piece is autobiography.

TEILHARD: In 1916 my mind was full of questions of how Christ would appear in the world should he vouchsafe to show himself. What would be his way of enfolding himself perceptibly in matter? What would be his impact on the things around him?

I was pondering this in a church near the front and at the same time looking at a painting of Christ on the walls. My eyes were wandering over the outlines of the painter's image, when suddenly I noticed that these very outlines were *melting.* Or at least *melting* is the best word I can think of. It seemed as though the surface that separated Christ from the world about him was changing into a film of vibration in which all limits were confounded. The transformation began near the borders of the portrait and spread from there until it embraced the whole contour. The vibrant atmosphere, which surrounded Christ with a halo, was not confined to the small space immediately about him, but it radiated to infinity. It was shot through by what appeared to be phosphorescent trails, tracing a continuous path of light as far as the outermost spheres of matter, making a sort of network of nerves throughout all the substance. *The whole universe vibrated*—and yet every *thing* in the universe remained clearly defined, its individuality still preserved. . . .

NARRATOR: "The outermost spheres of matter," "a network of nerves throughout all substance," "a universe vibrating"—how often Teilhard was to return to these points of his vision. Sometimes the few seconds of a vision take a lifetime to record. So it has often been with genius. So it was with Teilhard.

TEILHARD: The first war started me on the ladder. My essential ideas on the world and man dated from my time in the trenches. Under fire, a man is no longer the same man that he was sitting in a Paris bistro. War—at least war of the Fourteen-Eighteen variety—breaks the conventions, and I know that the reality I experienced in it as a stretcher bearer will be with me forever in the great task of understanding creation and how it must become more and more sanctified, how, O Lord, our work here follows you into your Kingdom, *opera sequuntur nostra.*

NARRATOR: So he returned to Paris to work once more on paleontology and prehistory. He began to lecture and the daring of his thought—

TEILHARD: We must dare all, we must dare all.

NARRATOR:—made a tremendous impact, especially upon the young generation. But his ideas of a threefold converging evolution—chemical, organic, psychosocial—later worked out with Edouard Le Roy—were far in advance of his time, and his superiors sent him to the Far East.

It was in effect banishment. But it enabled him to accumulate the data to prove his earlier theories. From now on he became a wanderer on the face of the earth.

TEILHARD: I begin to think the rest of my life will be like this, and death will find me still a wanderer.

NARRATOR: He was to spend months of his life traveling between one port and another.

TEILHARD: How many gulls have I seen, how many other people have seen them, without giving a thought to the mystery that accompanies their flight? How much rests on really *seeing*. Sometimes you look over the ship's rails and the water is dark. Then on another day you look down and the sea lights up as the prow cuts through the waves.

NARRATOR: In 1923 the destination was China and explorations of the interior.

TEILHARD: Look at these bleached bones of giraffes and antelopes that used to roam here thousands of years ago in the Miocene Age just as today they still roam in the tropical prairies of Africa. But you know, absorbed as I am in geology and fascinated as I am by bones, my interest is wandering farther afield. It is the *Other* that I now seek, the *Thing* across the gap, the *Thing* on the far side. "*Other*," "*Thing*"—how limiting language can be! But that's no excuse for us to give up.

NARRATOR: Later there were excavations in Ethiopia and journeys recorded with a quick eye for detail.

TEILHARD: I remember saying Christmas mass there. The servers had bare feet under their cassocks and a zebra skin served as an altar cloth.

NARRATOR: Or there were moments in India specially captured in letters for his lifelong friend, the Abbé Breuil.

TEILHARD: We went to look at the excavations at Mohenjo-Daro. More than three thousand years before our era, people were living there who played with dice like our own, fished with hooks like ours, and wrote in characters we can't read. We live surrounded by ideas and objects infinitely more ancient than we imagine; and yet at the same time everything is in motion.

NARRATOR: Long before this, ideas had become vision, and he now had an unfaltering sense of the harmony and unity of the whole creation. He came toward his end at ease both with time's immense duration and his own brief lifespan; rejoicing in both the vastness of space and the tiny universe within the atom. Full of confidence in the science of man and eager for the journey to point Omega where the human adventure will be fulfilled.

For this last stretch of his life, he was based in America. He was a man who had been always on the go. One month in Peking, the next in Hong Kong; one month in Malaya, the next in Honolulu; one month in Rangoon, and the next in New York. It was in New York that he died. Less than a month before he had said:

TEILHARD: When I die, I want to die on the Day of the Resurrection.

NARRATOR: On Easter morning after he had said his own mass he had gone to the high mass at St. Patrick's Cathedral. After it, he had walked through Central Park and enjoyed listening to the band. He lunched with several fathers of his own Order and was in excellent fettle. Later in the afternoon when he joined some more friends he confided to them:

TEILHARD: I've never had such a lovely Easter before.

NARRATOR: Then he walked over to the table—and fell, like a tree struck by lightning.

TEILHARD: What's happened—where am I?

NARRATOR: Within minutes his breathing had stopped. He was seventy-three. God had granted him his wish to die on the Day of the Resurrection. Yet in the world at large his name remained comparatively unknown. As he himself said during his life:

TEILHARD: I hardly expect to be listened to immediately. Yet once an idea has been launched, it will gather momentum. What we have to do is to broadcast the seed.

NARRATOR: That cue was to be followed much sooner than he supposed. Scarcely had he been laid in his grave than a distinguished committee of scientists and men of letters was formed to sponsor his works. The first of his books that the committee sponsored was *The Phenomenon of Man,* and within days over seventy thousand copies had been sold in France. Since then it has been translated widely and drawn fire of every kind. Teilhard's beginning point was man.

TEILHARD: . . . the whole phenomenon of man. I do not see man as a static center of the world, but as the axis and leading shoot of evolution, which is something far finer, because in you and me, through matter, the whole history of the world is in part reflected. The trouble, as I keep emphasizing, is that we don't look far enough. It's the old problem of seeing. We're continually inclined to isolate ourselves from the things and events that surround us, as though we were spectators looking at them from the outside, not elements in what's going on. If I say the word history, your mind probably races back six thousand years. That's at the most—and that's because you're thinking of history in terms of dates and recorded events. But when you see history in its proper perspective, it's far longer. In the history of the world's evolution thirty thousand years are like a flash. I have concentrated so much on the past, on the earliest phases of the universe before even man existed, because I believe it helps to give us surprising visions of the future. Man is no more static than the world, for he too, like the world, is evolving all the time.

In the books which I read as a boy, man was presented to me as an erratic object in a disjointed world, a conscious being standing like an actor before an unconscious backcloth. This is where I as a scientist felt bound to make a protest. I'm optimistic about man —and I'm not forgetting the bombs that were dropped on Nagasaki or Hiroshima. Let me say why. Nothing on earth will ever saturate our desire for knowledge, so that as we advance toward a human era of science, so we shall find it will be eminently an era of human science. You will have the paradox where man, the knowing subject, will perceive at last that man, the object of knowledge, is the key to the whole science of nature. In short, man is the solution of everything that we can know. To decipher man is to try and find out how our world was made and how it ought to go on making itself.

STUDENT: Aren't you allowing reason to supplant belief and to say that man is sufficient unto himself?

TEILHARD: Your question is a good one, sir. To every outward appearance, the modern world was born of anti-religious movement. In an essay that I'm writing . . .

NARRATOR: (Four times in *The Phenomenon* he refers to it as an essay.)

TEILHARD: . . . In this essay, I submit that the tension between science and faith should not be resolved in terms either of elimination or duality, but in terms of a synthesis. For neither can develop without the other. And the reason is simple: the same life animates both. Neither in its impetus nor its achievements can science go to its limits without becoming *tinged with mysticism and charged with faith.* Now a man will only continue to research so long as he is prompted by some passionate interest and this interest will be dependent on the conviction, strictly undemonstrable to science, that the universe has a direction. . . . Hence comes belief in progress, something that all scientific and religious thinkers accept. So much for research, which in another context I have called adoration. Likewise, direction implies eventual unification, an acceptance of the convergent properties of the world we belong to.

So, sooner or later, we run into the necessity of finding something that will associate our lives together without diminishing or distorting them. Hence comes belief in a supremely attractive center which has personality. Our friends in the last century were not wrong to refer to the "religion of science." Their error was not to see far enough. If they had, they would have realized that their cult of humanity implied the reintegration, in a renewed form, of those very forces which they claimed to be getting rid of. I would be a traitor to God and myself if I didn't emphasize for all I'm worth that religion and science are but phases of one and the same act of complete knowledge.

NARRATOR: The "act of complete knowledge." This was always his search. Not enough for him to count the grains of sand, to number the species of birds and insects. Throughout *The Phenomenon,* his vision relates the individual story to the great pattern of genesis. How superbly his words capture the half-million insects imprisoned in their unchanging plane of life.

TEILHARD: A multitude pathetically involved in a blind alley.

NARRATOR: Or at the other extreme, there are the huge mammals, the mammals that grew so big they became immobile.

TEILHARD: How as children we delighted when we read of them as dragons, or wondered at them when we saw their skeletons presented to us in famous natural history museums.

NARRATOR: Or there are the birds that radiated into over eight thousand different species. They specialized in flying and their growth led to fragmentation. But in the primates such as monkeys . . .

TEILHARD: . . . evolution went straight to work on the brain. They alone have the aura of freedom.

NARRATOR: But in all the exciting phases of the creation, it is *man alone who remains a single species.* Men are also migrants. But on a round planet they keep meeting, they intermarry, interbreed— communication is inevitable. Human convergence, a coming together of human thought, is taking place at every moment. The pattern has always been there. It was only a case of looking.

TEILHARD: You ask why I'm so happy, my friend? It's because the earth is round.

NARRATOR: Sometimes his answers could be as simple as that. At others, he had to invent new terms to explain his ideas. By noosphere, he meant a layer of thought which *we* by our conscious thinking spread over the universe.

TEILHARD: Something quite as real as the atmosphere.

NARRATOR: Or, there's Teilhard's point Omega. Call this if you like the top of a pyramid, a focal point where the material and the spiritual converge, where, as Saint Paul says, "God shall be all in all." In point Omega lies all the journey from Alpha, or put another way: In the ending lies the beginning, or "In the beginning was the Word. . . ." Teilhard, like another Jesuit, Gerard Manley Hopkins, had a sympathy for Duns Scotus' philosophy, just as both

men, like so many mystics before them, had a natural predilection
for Saint Paul and Saint John the Beloved Apostle. A case may
be made of poet speaking to poet across the centuries. Certainly it
was far from his intention to produce another *Summa Theologica*.
Rather, if a link is needed, the right one perhaps is Langland's
cosmic *Vision of Piers Plowman*. For he too looked at the incarnate
God—in Christ alloyed with earth—and saw the whole of human
life converging in him.

[*Pause*]

Photographs of Teilhard show a finely drawn face, weathered by
wind and sea. There's a glint in his eyes that can only be called
daredevil. Professor George Barbour, an American Presbyterian of
Scottish descent, paints this picture of him in the field.

GEORGE BARBOUR: It was my privilege to be in the field with Père
Teilhard on four continents—eastern Asia, California, France, and
the Transvaal. On these expeditions he usually wore a khaki drill
suit of military cut with four pockets—the upper ones for pencil,
pen, cigarettes and matches, and the lower pair for the little black
notebooks and his breviary. . . . Often, riding a Mongolian pony,
he would spy a reworked stone implement fifteen feet away, where
others saw nothing but a spread of pebbles. . . . He was always an
ideal companion. During the day he would concentrate strictly on
the project in hand, but at night he would relax and talk freely
about the ideas close to his heart: the problem of overpopulation,
the nature of true peace, the link between progress and religion.
. . . Once in China, Pierre was sitting on some stone steps when
a mule kicked out savagely. The blow broke a blood vessel and
within a few minutes he had a dark blister the size of an egg right
over the temporal artery. That night I kept Pierre's temple cool
with constant compresses and read to him his breviary. It was a
wonderful experience.

On another occasion I recall that we were fording a river that was
so deep we had to cross half-naked with our clothes and shoes in a
bundle over our shoulders. I was ahead of Pierre, sufficiently ahead
to be able to catch him on the last twenty feet of my ciné camera,
half-stripped and washing off the mud. I left China before it could

be developed, and it lay for two years in the Cenozoic Laboratory in Peking before reaching me in New York. When I showed it to Pierre fifteen years later, he remarked: "Do you think *my Father General*, if he saw this, mightn't consider me to have been unfrocked prematurely?"

NARRATOR: *The Phenomenon of Man* had a mixed reception. Sir Julian Huxley wrote a preface for the English edition praising his old friend, but finally resisting its complete vision. Professor P. B. Medawar attacked it in the January, 1961 number of *Mind*.

P. B. MEDAWAR: The greater part of it is nonsense, tricked out by a variety of tedious metaphysical conceits, in the tradition of *Naturphilosophie*, a philosophical indoor pastime of German origin— tipsy euphoric prose-poetry which is one of the more tiresome manifestations of the French spirit. . . . In his lay capacity Teilhard, a naturalist, practiced a comparatively humble and unexacting science.

NARRATOR: Professor Medawar goes on to say that Teilhard has no grasp of the real weakness of modern evolutionary theory. Canon Charles Raven, however, is inclined to think, on the evidence of Professor Medawar's more recent Herbert Spencer lecture, that the Professor has only just learned what evolution means to French scientists and puts forward as his own an evolutionary process in three phases, chemical, organic and psychosocial, which was set out in great detail in 1927 by Teilhard and his friend, the philosopher Edouard Le Roy.

Canon Raven himself only came upon the work of Teilhard some five years ago, but he recognized at once a fellow spirit, and in his book on Teilhard he writes of him as one of the few men who opened new vistas for him in the universe.

CANON CHARLES RAVEN: The trouble is that most of us are still living in two—or if you like—two-and-twenty different worlds. So we contradict the whole trend both of religion and of science: we deny the unity of the cosmos, its wholeness, its pattern, its progress.

When, fifty years ago, I had to choose between research in Christian doctrine and Mendelian genetics, the two seemed (and in fact were) in head-on collision. I have worked happily in both fields; and seen basic changes. But the cleavage is still obvious, and is a chief source of our lack of any public philosophy and the chaos of our aesthetic, moral, personal, social, and international behavior.

Of all modern men Pierre Teilhard de Chardin has in my opinion best "seen life steadily, seen it whole"—seen it from the double standpoint material and spiritual, stereoscopically and in true perspective. He was greatly gifted by heredity and home; educated as an eminent paleontologist and a Catholic priest; tested by five years of front-line warfare from Ypres to Verdun; experienced by many friendships and world-wide travel; and in character, as his closest comrade, and masses of others describe him: "of all men I have known certainly the noblest." Although forbidden to publish his work, he has left us a coherent and contemporary interpretation of the creative process, of the present crisis, and of our future religious and secular program.

Two recent events underline his importance. The first is the demonstrations of the unity and interdependence of all the elements of the cosmos by new discoveries in atomic physics completing our picture of basic structure, and in submolecular chemistry exploring the whole field of organic life and illuminating our knowledge both of its structure and its functioning as in heredity and memory, and establishing a psychosomatic view of the universe. The second is the new insights of man's sense perceptions—insights which demonstrate the flagrant defects of the current Freudian analysis, and may well interpret what we now call extrasensory perception—a subject of which in his last years Teilhard recognized the importance.

Nothing so far as I am aware has happened to upset or seriously challenge Teilhard's vision. Much, and I would include Professor P. B. Medawar's conversion, has confirmed it—not least the records of the Vatican Council.

NARRATOR: So the debate goes on. Some theologians have reservations about *The Phenomenon*. Among them is Father Cornelius Ernst, the Dominican theologian.

FATHER CORNELIUS ERNST: Well, for instance, take the matter of "time" and "time" as implied in Father Teilhard's vision. Expressions he used such as "a single process of convergent evolution from the creation of the Universe to its culmination at Omega point." Now in the Christian theology of "time," the end event, the last event, has already taken place by expiation in the life, death, and resurrection of Jesus Christ. So that the time before Jesus Christ and the time after him cannot form a simple progression, as it were a kind of single line. Our time really is the time of the sacraments. Each time we celebrate the Eucharist, for instance, the past—the death and resurrection of Christ: the future—the coming again of Christ—these two are brought together in a simultaneous "now": the "now" of the risen Christ: so that in every Eucharist then, the past, present, and future are brought together.

And then secondly, this vision of the single continuous ascent seems to do violence to the delicate balance of nature and grace in Christian theology. It's extremely difficult to see how Father Teilhard's universe evolving in a single triumphant sweep, according to the law of a generalized biology, can possibly allow God's grace to be grace and indeed man's sin to be sin. Father Teilhard's views about sin are not generally thought to be very profound.

I don't want to seem dismissive about Father Teilhard. I'm quite prepared to grant his seriousness as a . . . well, as a visionary, someone who has contributed to our "fund" of human experience: but I do want to distinguish this contribution from its theological orthodoxy. That vision of Father Teilhard's, however much it contributes to our sense of what it is to be human, needs to be criticized.

NARRATOR: Philosophers are also divided about the value of Teilhard's thought. Father John Russell, the Jesuit philosopher, is a supporter.

FATHER JOHN RUSSELL: The situation which Teilhard entered was one in which materialists asserted that everything in this world is governed by blind purposeless determinism; while Christians too often were simply fighting a rear-guard action against them—trying to resist as long as possible any scientific theory which seemed to conflict with traditional ideas. Teilhard could not be content with such a negative attitude. For him the world was essentially a manifestation of God's plan. It was essentially orientated, first, toward the production of man, and ultimately, toward God himself.

He held that matter has within itself an innate tendency toward the production of higher, more complex, and more perfect structures. So that from simple inorganic bodies more complex ones can be produced. These in turn, under suitable conditions, can become living. Simple organisms can evolve into complex ones, culminating in man. And he believed that even in man the same law obtains —waiting to form more complex societies which in turn cannot rest at a purely human level. The ultimate goal of the process must be something higher: the union of man with God through Jesus Christ.

So Teilhard's vision of the unity of the physical world on the one hand, and of its holiness on the other; its involvement with God's plans for mankind; does seem to me to have a profound significance for all of us who believe in the value of both matter and spirit; of both science and religion.

NARRATOR: Father Martin Jarrett-Kerr of the Mirfield Community of the Resurrection has translated a book on Teilhard. He has studied not only the writings of Teilhard, but the writings about him.

FATHER MARTIN JARRETT-KERR: I first came across Teilhard's work— I had never heard of his name at all—when I happened to be in New York in 1957. I met there a French lady in the diplomatic service and, interestingly enough, she was also a Catholic and connected with Dorothy Day's Catholic Worker movement—a rather left-wing group of Catholics in New York. She gave me *The Phenomenon* because she thought that I might be interested in it. I read a bit of it and became fascinated, and took it back with me to South Africa where I was actually working. There I became even more interested in it. Of course, Teilhard himself had been to South Africa in his paleontological work, and this seemed to tie up. Then curiously enough, not long after that, I came across another piece of evidence of Teilhard's considerable influence in Africa. This was a work by Leopold Senghor, the President of Senegal, in which he describes how as a young student in Paris he was very much attracted to Marxism, but somehow felt that it was both too Western a phenomenon and one that made him deny his African heritage. For a long time he was looking around for a philosophy and then, although he was not a Christian—he was in fact Muslim—he came across the works of Teilhard de Chardin. They seemed to make sense of his "Africanism," his desire for *négritude,* for the African personality. They gave him a philosophy in which all this seemed to have some significance. So those are two reasons why I found the work interesting.

But if you want a brief resumé of why I think Teilhard's work is of very great seminal importance, I would say something like this. That Teilhard, all the time, was talking out of two sides of his mouth. Out of one side of his mouth he was talking to his fellow scientists and he was saying to them, "As scientists you've got to take notice of this strange phenomenon of man himself." Then, out of the other side, he was saying to Christians, "Science is an expression of part of God's purpose for man. You've got to take science seriously as a Christian."

NARRATOR: Cardinal Koenig of Vienna has, perhaps, indicated the most profitable attitude toward the seed-bed of ideas which Teilhard's work provides. The Cardinal accepts Teilhard's word, noosphere, the realm of mind, collective and individual, as the goal of human aspiration.

CARDINAL KOENIG: Positive evidence will be necessary to prove that agreement can be reached between the scientific conception of the world and of man, and religion. The Jesuit, Teilhard de Chardin, has gone further than anyone else in dedicating himself to this task. For many years, he has struggled to define the bridge between science and faith, in the same way as he has, as an anthropologist and priest, united the scientific conception of man. In his bold vision, he sees the resurgence of a humanity which will find its own happiness in the noosphere. This will not be attained by automation alone, but by the united desire of all who desire progress.

[*Pause*]

NARRATOR: For Teilhard the mass was the highest form of Christian prayer. Let us eavesdrop on a sermon that he preached on New Year's Day, 1932, before he set out on an expedition to cross Turkistan and Mongolia. His congregation was as mixed as those who have been quoted and who have taken part in this program.

TEILHARD: My dear friends, here we are to begin this New Year in the face of God. God, no doubt, has not the same precise meaning, the same face, for each of us. But because we are all men, none of us can escape the sense that there exists a higher energy, in which we must recognize—since it is higher—the enlarged equivalent of our own intelligence and will. It is in this powerful *Presence* that we should be recollected for a moment, at the beginning of this year. We ask this Presence to crown our enterprise with success.

NARRATOR: But sometimes on these expeditions there was no wine or bread to be found—and mass could not be said. Teilhard would then kneel on the earth and say:

TEILHARD: O Lord, since I have neither bread, nor wine, nor altar, I your priest, on the altar of the whole earth, offer you the toil and sorrow of the world. . . . Receive me, O Lord, a victim which creation, drawn by your power, offers up to you in today's new dawn. Bread, our toil, is in itself, I know, no more than a vast dismemberment. Wine, too, our sorrow, is alas, no more than a draught that dissolves; but in the heart of this formless mass of earth, you have planted an irresistible and sanctifying urge which makes each one of us, from the godless man to the man of faith, cry out, "Lord, make us to be one."